895

Behold the angels of soul qualities
Colors of attributes right within your soul
Listen to the angels of purifying qualities
Their rays will open your soul's door

Seven Mansions
of Color

by
Alex Jones

DeVorss & Company
P.O. Box 550, Marina del Rey, CA 90294

*To my friend, the Lion of Bengal,
and my mother and father who made
this book possible*

*Special thanks to Ann Emerson
for her editorial work*

Author's Note

THE FUNDAMENTAL INTENTION in the writing of this book is to prove the basic oneness of the mystical experiences of east and west through the instrumentality of the universal color rays emanating from the White Light of Spirit. I have also documented the oneness of all religions through the manifestation of the qualities of the color rays in the lives of the saints and sages of all spiritual disciplines.

My experience and main emphasis in the use of color has been through the power of mind. By using techniques of color meditation and color breathing one's consciousness is developed and discords are harmonized. This results in a direct connection between color and consciousness so that individuals can use their own inner potential to heal themselves in body, mind and soul.

I am primarily a spiritual writer and work predominantly in this domain. I am not a physician, nor have I had any formal medical training. I do not claim to be an authority in the kind of color healing which uses lamps and other mechanical devices, nor do I diagnose and prescribe colors for different physical ailments. I am not proficient in these practices. Any references to the use of color in treating specific physical diseases in this book come from the experiments of other researchers and authors listed in the bibliography.

As mentioned in the chapter on Color and World Cycles, we have just entered the Dwapara Yuga. In this age, healing by color will become the accepted norm of treatment. Since we have just entered this cycle, the apparent healing properties of color are being rediscovered. Extensive scientific clinical research and experimentation still need to be carried out to prove and justify many medical claims.

No two souls are alike; each will respond to color uniquely. The characteristics of intelligent color energies are given; their laws are universal. Some people may require more of one color than another, or they may need a combination of several colors. I am not prescribing different colors for different ailments, but giving the properties of colors. It is the responsibility of each person to learn his or her own color needs. It is in the discovering that one will also find healing. Those who practice these methods are themselves the healers and take responsibility for their own diagnoses and treatments.

It is my hope that you may gain an appreciation for the essence of colors and use their qualities in your daily life. It is also my hope that you may gain a greater appreciation for the creator and co-ordinator of color—The Supreme Master Artist.

Contents

1. **Dancing Vibrations on the Screen of Space**   **1**

2. **The Spectrum of Consciousness**   **6**

3. **Mental and Emotional Attributes of the Divine Rays**   **15**

    The Red Level of Consciousness   15

    The Orange Level of Consciousness   16

    The Yellow Level of Consciousness   18

    The Green Level of Consciousness   20

    The Blue Level of Consciousness   22

    The Indigo Level of Consciousness   24

    The Violet Level of Consciousness   27

    The White Light of Spirit   31

4. **Overcoming Psychological Problems with the Divine Rays**   **36**

    Treating Psychological Problems Through the Color Rays   36

    The Red Ray (Coccygeal Center)   37

    The Orange Ray (Sacral Center)   38

The Yellow Ray (Lumbar or Solar
    Plexus Center)   40

The Green Ray (Dorsal or Heart Center)   42

The Blue Ray (Cervical or Throat Center)   43

The Indigo Ray (Medulla and Spiritual
    Eye Center)   44

The Violet Ray (Thousand-Petaled Lotus Center)   44

5. Spiritual Unfoldment of the Divine Rays   **46**

The One Journey of all Religions   46

The First Church or Mansion (Coccygeal Center)   49

The Second Church or Mansion (Sacral Center)   51

The Third Church or Mansion (Lumbar Center)   52

The Fourth Church or Mansion (Dorsal Center)   53

The Fifth Church or Mansion (Cervical Center)   55

The Sixth Church or Mansion (Medulla and
    Spiritual Eye Center)   56

The Seventh Church or Mansion (Thousand-
    Petaled Lotus Center)   58

Inner Experiences of the Seven Mansions   60

The Seven Mansions (Seven Color Rays)   61

The Elements and Inner Sounds Manifesting
    in the Seven Mansions   62

Inner Realizations of the Seven Mansions
    (Seven Color Rays)   64

Other Manifestations of the Divine Rays,
    According to Patanjali   65

Visions of the Seven Mansions (Seven Color Rays)   66

6. The Color Attributes of the World Cycles   **69**

Evolutionary Cycles and Their Colors   69

The Red Cycle (Bhuloka—Kali Yuga)   72

The Orange Cycle (Bhuvarloka—Dwapara Yuga)   72

The Yellow Cycle (Swarloka—Treta Yuga)   72

The Green Cycle (Maharloka—Satya Yuga)   73

The Blue Cycle (Janaloka—Satya Yuga)   73

The Indigo Cycle (Tapoloka—Satya Yuga)   73

The Violet Cycle (Satyaloka—Satya Yuga)   74

7. Color and the Arts   **75**

Color and Music   75

Color and Art   78

8. The Physical Expression of the Divine Rays   **81**

The Physical Essence   81

The Rays   83

9. Physical Properties of Color   **86**

Radiant and Pigment Colors   86

Color Terminology   91

Color Characteristics and Relationships   92

Color Response   96

Color Preference   97

Color Schemes in the Home   98

Color in Industry   98

Color in the Wardrobe   100

Healing Properties of the Spectrum of
    Physical Colors   101

Individual Color Propensities   106
    Red, Orange, Yellow, Green, Blue, Indigo,
    Violet, White, Ultra-violet, Magenta, Purple,
    Turquoise, Lemon, Scarlet.

10. **Methods of Treatment**   **123**

Meditation on the White Light   124

Meditation on Color   126

Color Breathing   127

Sunlight and Artificial Rays from Lamps   128

Color-Charged Water   129

Foods and Their Color Essences   130

Gem Therapy   132

Color and Chemical Elements   132

Bibliography   **135**

1

Dancing Vibrations on the Screen of Space

CREATION AND ALL its various manifestations are vibrating to various colors. Vibration is a force of motion and
the frequency of the moving molecules determines its radiant
color. All vibrations—from the thoughts we think to those given
off by inorganic substances—are scintillating with their own
unique individual color. Not only do all vibrations have their
own particular color; they are also endowed with a unique
sound and a guiding intelligence is present within their atomic
structures. When we come to look upon everything we en-
counter as being endowed with a unique quality, with intelligence, color and sound, we gain a new and exhilarating per-
spective on life. Each particle of space is an altar to which we
may bow with respect as a special manifestation of the creative
energy of Spirit. We can behold all of creation as a multicolored
spectacle projected on the screen of space.

In order to understand the marvel of color and consciousness we need to understand how creation was manifested. In
the beginning God existed alone as Spirit, the One Absolute
Unmanifested Consciousness.[1] Spirit then desired to create
and so It conceived the universe in Its consciousness as a mul-
titude of thoughts and ideas. As waves on an ocean cannot
exist without a wind, so Spirit agitated the calm ocean of Its
consciousness with the storm of creativity to produce the waves
of countless thoughts. With the creation of the Law of Relativity or Law of Opposites,[2] divisions seem to appear in the

1

one indivisible Spirit.³ Supreme Intelligence created the idea of change or time and the idea of particles—the innumerable atoms. By these acts of creation all particles are bestowed with a feeling of individuality and separateness from the one Divine Source, God. As the many sprinklers of a fountain are sustained by the one common water supply, so the many facets of creation are created and sustained by God.

Spirit further unfolded the drama of creation when It desired to transmute Its cosmic play of ideas into tangible form. In order to crystalize the elements already created as ideas, It vibrated upon them and projected them with will and almighty force. Spirit thus created the beam of pure White Light or Intelligent Cosmic Energy. "Let there be Light and there was Light."⁴ The Cosmic Beam of Spirit contains two natures: the finer vibrations of consciousness and the grosser vibrations of potential matter.

God the Father is Spirit, the One Supreme Intelligence existing beyond vibratory creation. The Son is the Christ Consciousness⁵ or Christ Intelligence which is the unblemished, reflected consciousness of God the Father existing within vibratory creation. The Christ Consciousness manifests undisturbed within each atom and is the governing power that guides all creation. Mother Nature proclaims the natural law of rhythm and balance, the cycles of co-operation between Her various forces and elements. There is an awe-inspiring intelligence that guides the tiny seed to grow into a mighty tree. The rainy seasons come to sprout the seeds; the sun fills them with life-sustaining energy.

The ultimate conclusion of many great scientists from their inner and outer investigations is that there is a great intelligence guiding this cosmic universe. That great intelligence is guiding all activities if we would only look to see it. That intelligence is the Christ Consciousness in every atom of creation, which Jesus and all liberated Sons of God became one with and manifested in their own consciousnesses.

The Holy Ghost is the basic, creative vibration from which all other grosser vibrations manifest. The Christ Consciousness guides the vibratory structure of creation through the manifesting creative power of the Holy Ghost. Streams of energy rays of different vibratory power descend from the Holy Ghost to build, sustain and renew different aspects of creation. The Holy Ghost upholds the universe by vibration and also has a sound, depicting its activity. That sound is the Amen of the Christians, Jews, Romans, Greeks, and Egyptians; the Aum (OM) of the Hindus and Yogis; Hum of the Tibetans; and Amin of the Moslems. Everything in the universe is contained within the Holy Ghost. The pure White Light of the Holy Ghost or Amen is the sum total of all the colors and sounds of the universe.

Cosmic Light or Energy created the finer energies and forces of atoms, electrons, life force, electricity, rays and so on of the astral realm.[6] These finer forces cannot be detected by the usual five senses of perception. Space or firmament is a vibratory sphere created by Spirit to separate the astral realm from the physical. The physical realm is the Light of Spirit solidified. It is the grossest expression of God's Cosmic Energy. It is made up of the elements of earth, water, fire, air and ether and these basic components have arranged themselves into the ninety-odd elements of the physical universe. Science tells us that first came the electrons, nebulae, ocean, dry land, vegetation, animals and finally man. The electrons of which the universe is made are the dispersed White Light of Spirit. These dancing particles of energy have formed themselves into the subtle astral realm and the grosser physical realm.

The universe is, in essence, not matter but mind—the countless thoughts of God materialized. When man dreams, he is aware of the material objects which he has created in his thoughts. During the dream state his consciousness is fully alive as he experiences different emotions and when he awakens he knows what he has dreamed. Through man's thought, will and power of visualization he projects a dream movie on the screen of his subconscious mind. The Great Dreamer is also dreaming the grand drama of creation and is projecting His dream on the screen of space for our entertainment. We perceive the cosmic dream drama through the five senses of sight, smell, taste, hearing and touch on the screen of our consciousnesses. And so we can see that everything in the universe is really the thoughts of God materialized at different rates of color and sound vibration.

Our perceptions are limited by the five senses and we can see and hear only a segment of the vast range of frequencies of color and sound. If we learn to awaken the intuitive faculty within, we can come to experience the colors and sounds of the astral world. By deeper meditation we may come in contact with the basic vibration of the Holy Ghost or the Cosmic, Intelligent Vibration of Light. Through refinement of our consciousnesses we may become one with the Light of God and realize that creation is but a play of light and shadow and that we are a holy thought of God.

Notes—Chapter 1

1. "Where no sun or moon or fire shines, that is My Supreme Abode . . ." —Bhagavad-Gita XV:6

Note: The Bhagavad-Gita ("Song of the Lord") is the Hindu Bible which is part of the Mahabharata. Within its pages are the sacred sayings of Lord Krishna compiled millenniums ago by the sage Vyasa.

2. The Law of Relativity is present everywhere in creation: heat and cold, light and shadow, pleasure and pain and so on.

3. "When a man beholds all separate beings as existent in the One that has expanded Itself into the many, he merges with Brahma." —Bhagavad-Gita XIII:31

4. Genesis I:3

5. Christ Consciousness: The awareness of the Cosmic Intelligence of Spirit in every atom of vibratory creation.

6. Astral realm: The subtle sphere of light and color composed of prana. A sphere where those with higher spiritual consciousness reside after death for further lessons. Beyond the astral is the causal or ideational sphere. (See chapter 43 of *Autobiography of a Yogi* by Paramahansa Yogananda for more details on the astral realm and astral bodies.)

2

The Spectrum of Consciousness

Not only is there a physical spectrum of colors from our solar source the sun; there is also the astral spectrum of Cosmic Rays emanating from the White Light of Spirit. Let us explore how the Cosmic Rays descend into our consciousnesses and structure and maintain our bodies, minds, and souls. Surrounding the human body we have an electromagnetic field known as the aura. This has been photographed by the Russians through Kirlian photography and seen through Kilner[1] screens or glasses. It is through the aura by our will power that we draw the energy of God into our causal, astral and physical bodies. Christ said, "Man shall not live by bread alone but by every word that proceedeth out of the mouth of God."[2] The word of God is the Holy Cosmic Energy which enters the body through the medulla oblongata. This point of intake is called the mouth of God and is located at the base of the brain where the back of the skull is connected to the neck.

The three main channels that carry the prana or life energy in the body are called the Ida, Pingala and Susumna. These current channels are inside our subtle astral body rather than in the gross physical one. From the medulla the Cosmic Energy goes into each of these channels to sustain the body. The most important of the three is the Susumna. It receives a ceaseless stream of Cosmic Energy which is sent to the thousand-petaled lotus or crown chakra for storage and then relayed to the different lower chakra centers to carry on the various functions of the body. The Ida carries life current through the left side of the body. The Pingala carries life current through the right side of the body. The Susumna channel carries life current in the middle of the spine. The Ida rules the left nostril and supplies energy to all the organs and systems on the left side. The Pingala rules the right nostril and supplies energy to all the organs on the right side. The Pingala sends energy to the right lung and right brain hemisphere, whereas the Ida supplies the left. Wherever the Ida, Pingala and Susumna come together in the body they form a chakra center. There are six chakra centers in the body where the three currents converge. The crown is a separate chakra.

The Cosmic Life Force is the current that directly sustains the body and all other sources of energy are secondary. The food we eat gives us some energy, but what energy and intelligence helps digest our food and makes use of the nutrients? There is a ray of life force—an intelligent energy—that coordinates the transformation of the food we eat into energy so that it is usable by the body.

This specialized energy is a unique ray emanating from the Cosmic Current and brought into the body through the medulla oblongata. As the Cosmic Energy descends down the Susumna it splits into seven separate currents, one for each chakra. Each chakra is a distributor of life force which has a particular function in the body. The seven chakras or seven cerebrospinal centers are represented symbolically as the seven candlesticks and churches mentioned in Revelations. The seven centers are also indicated by the seven mansions that Saint Teresa of Avila[3] talks about in her book *The Interior Castle*. These candlesticks or churches are the thousand-petaled lotus or crown chakra in the brain—medulla oblongata and its polar opposite, the spiritual eye, cervical or throat, dorsal or heart, lumbar or solar plexus, sacral and the coccygeal center at the base of the

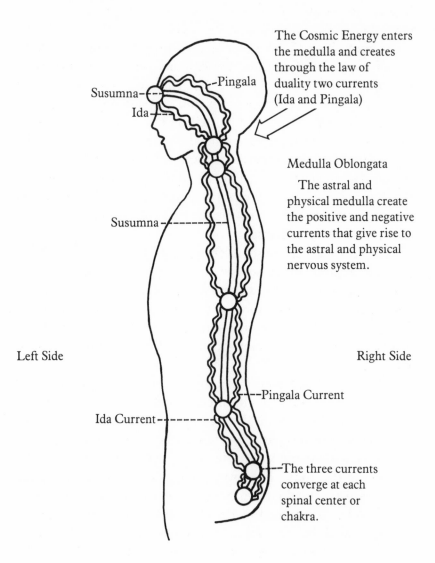

The Cosmic Energy enters
the medulla and creates
through the law of
duality two currents
(Ida and Pingala)

Medulla Oblongata

   The astral and
physical medulla create
the positive and negative
currents that give rise to
the astral and physical
nervous system.

Pingala

Susumna—

Ida—

Susumna—

Left Side

Right Side

—Pingala Current

Ida Current—

—The three currents
converge at each
spinal center or
chakra.

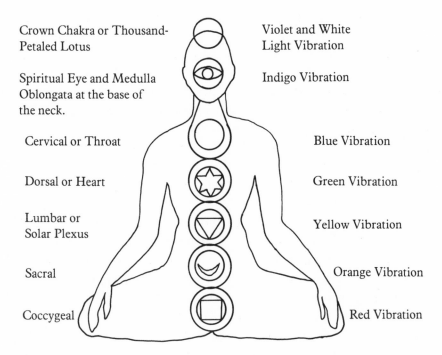

Crown Chakra or Thousand-Petaled Lotus — Violet and White Light Vibration

Spiritual Eye and Medulla Oblongata at the base of the neck. — Indigo Vibration

Cervical or Throat — Blue Vibration

Dorsal or Heart — Green Vibration

Lumbar or Solar Plexus — Yellow Vibration

Sacral — Orange Vibration

Coccygeal — Red Vibration

spine. The entire chakra system acts like a prism which separates the Cosmic White Light into the spectrum of seven life forces.

Each individualized chakra has a particular vibratory manifestation which is attuned to a different ray of life force from the Cosmic Current. The specialized rays are absorbed and reradiated into the body and aura by the chakras. The color ray for each chakra is as follows: red for the coccygeal, orange for the sacral, yellow for the lumbar, green for the dorsal, blue for the cervical, indigo for the medulla oblongata and spiritual eye and violet and White Light for the crown or thousand-petaled lotus in the brain.

Do not think of these colors as physical, for they are astral colors and can be seen only by those who have developed clairvoyant or spiritual sight. These Cosmic Rays are reflected in the aura according to how they are absorbed and reradiated by the chakras. If the chakras are open and functioning properly, allowing the full potential of the Cosmic Rays to pass through, then there will be bright, clear colors in the aura. If a person's chakras are blocked, then the vibration that will manifest will be a dull and muddy color. Each person is responsible for his or her auric colors which are a result of the sum total of all the efforts toward purification in this life and past incarnations.[4] The vibrations of one's body—the vibrating atoms, molecules, cells, organs, and systems—all contribute to one's auric color. A person's thoughts, moods, feelings and attitudes also manifest themselves in the aura.

Man relates mainly to three bodies: the physical, astral and causal.[5] The electromagnetic field or aura in the astral and causal bodies have seven bands which correspond to the seven energy levels or Cosmic Color Rays. In eastern religion the auric divisions are known as the material or Tatwic Aura, Prana, Karmic Sheath, Lower Manas (Mind), Higher Manas (Mind), Buddhic Sheath, and the Auric Egg. The Tatwic Aura is known in western metaphysics as the Etheric Aura which indicates the vibrational essence of the physical body. In the etheric or health aura we can determine physical problems before they come into existence in the physical body by noticing cloudy spots near the troubled area. If there is disease in the physical body, the normal lines of radiation of the etheric aura appear dropped and bent. This auric field draws in energy from the atmosphere and distributes it to the entire physical body. The astral—emotional—aura or Karmic Sheath is always changing in color with one's thoughts and moods. Nothing colors the astral aura more than habitual thought. If a person is constantly negative, he is in trouble. By negative thinking, feeling and acting he creates dark patches and dirty, muddy colors in the aura which prevent the flow of God's Creative Energy from reaching him. If he blocks out the Light of God by his self-created negation, his body will manifest various inharmonies. No one can live without the Light of God. No amount of filling the body with the outward sources of energy —ultraviolet rays of the sun, food, vitamins, minerals and liquids—will be able to help. The body is sustained primarily and principally by the Cosmic Current, and the outward sources of energy are only secondary.

One's true essence or state of consciousness can be determined by the predominant color in one's aura. There will be many changing colors but the color that remains consistent indicates one's essential nature or personality. If the predominant color is muddy, then that person needs to strive to perfect himself and discontinue manifesting negative qualities or thinking negative thoughts. The Cosmic Color Rays are always pure and undistorted in nature. When one manifests negative qualities within, they block out and hinder the positive essences of the rays, keeping them from saturating one's being. If you shine a pure yellow beam through a dirty glass window, then the color manifesting on the other side will be a dirty yellow. The same is true of one's aura.

The purpose of existence is to tune in with the Cosmic Color Rays and allow their power to manifest in one's life. Not only is it necessary to absorb the Cosmic Color Rays; it is also necessary to reradiate their perfect essences. In ordinary man these chakras or wheels of light are about two inches in diameter and spin just enough to bring in the required energy for living. In the spiritual masters of all religions, however, these same chakras are swirling balls of light like luminous suns drawing in the full potential of God's Cosmic Energy and reflecting that energy to all mankind.

Meditation is the most effective way to open up one's consciousness to receive these rays and to fully manifest them. By concentrating on the spinal centers and visualizing the Cosmic Color Rays flowing through them and saturating the body with energy, we can gradually perfect ourselves. It is a matter of attitude, acceptance and faith; it is also a definite scientific technique that opens the door to allow the Spirit of God to enter. Through deep meditation one begins to hear the Holy Ghost and see the White Light of Spirit. When this happens we begin to uplift the vibration of every cell of the body so it may become one with the Cosmic Current and manifest each ray to its fullest potential.

By developing one's will and concentrating on the medulla oblongata, we can learn to take in infinite supplies of energy. The more we concentrate on the inexhaustible supply of Cosmic Energy and bring it into our consciousness, the less fatigue we will feel. In time we will realize that our true nature is fatigueless, tireless, unlimited Cosmic Energy. Christ proclaimed this truth when he said, "The light of the body is the eye: if therefore thine eye be single, thy whole body shall be full of light."[6] A deeply meditating person will experience the White Light of God in the spiritual eye or ajna chakra. The spiritual eye is the polar opposite of the medulla oblongata and by concentrating one's energy and consciousness at this point, the Light of God will be revealed.

If one's attention is directed to each chakra center in turn, it is also possible to see each individual Color Ray appear in the spiritual eye. The more we become in tune with these divine energies, the more we will be able to control our destinies and live rich and rewarding lives. All mental, emotional and bodily diseases are a result of disharmony in vibrations. Since the body is made up of different rates of vibration or motion, all that is necessary to correct a particular malady is to bring the vibrations that are out of harmony into proper alignment or frequency.

Each Color Ray of energy passing through the different chakras has infinite qualities and attributes. They operate on the physical, mental and spiritual planes of existence. By controlling and perfecting each ray, inner divine realizations will be revealed to us of divine magnetic soul qualities and hidden latent powers. By being in attunement with a particular ray and its qualities, we will learn to be master of our emotions, moods and thoughts. Negative, unwanted habits will be transformed into positive soul qualities, and our inner diamond personality will shine forth radiant as the sun. We can learn to be masters of our own destiny and all elements will yield to us.

Saints of every religion who have achieved God realization through self-effort have manifested these qualities and attributes of Spirit. When we talk about perfection we mean perfecting all levels of consciousness—body, mind and soul. We need to learn to perfect each color. All colors are necessary; there are none higher or lower, for we need them all so that they all work in harmony to fulfill the Will of God.

Let us examine each Color Ray in turn to get an awareness of its divine blessings. In the next chapter we will explore the mental and emotional qualities of the rays and how they manifest in our lives. In the chapters following we will learn how to tune in with the physical functions of the rays and how we may use their energies to bring about healing and rejuvenation. We will also look into the spiritual essences of the rays. As we open each spinal center, we can have various spiritual experiences as we seek inwardly for the Divine Creative Essence of the Universe.

Notes—Chapter 2

1. Kilner, Dr. W.J.: A practitioner of St. Thomas Hospital, London who developed the 'dicyanin screen'; a lens painted with a coal-tar dye. The screen enables the eye to perceive the ultraviolet range of frequencies.

2. Matthew 4:4

3. Saint Teresa of Avila, 1515–1582; Spanish mystic and founder of the reformed order of Carmelites.

4. "Their thoughts immersed in That (Spirit), their souls one with Spirit, their sole allegiance and devotion given to Spirit, their beings purified from poisonous delusion by the antidote of wisdom—such men reach the state of nonreturn." Bhagavad-Gita V:17

5. Astral body: Made of light or prana, it is the seat of man's mental and emotional natures. It is composed of ninteen elements: intelligence, ego, feeling, mind (sense-consciousness); five instruments of life force.

Causal body: The causal body is composed of 35 idea elements which are the idea-matrix for the 19 elements of the astral body plus the 16 elements of the physical body. (See chapter 43 of *Autobiography of a Yogi* by Paramahansa Yogananda for more details on the causal and astral realm and bodies).

6. Matthew 6:22

3

Mental and Emotional Attributes of the Divine Rays

THE RED LEVEL OF CONSCIOUSNESS

THE GREAT MASTERS of all religions have come to earth to fulfill a special, divine mission. They have been way-showers to all souls in how to bring themselves back to a state of perfection—which is oneness with God. They have shown us the way of truth not so much by their words, but more by their example. They practiced what they taught, and by following their example we can achieve liberation.

The Red Cosmic Ray symbolizes life, strength, power and vitality. Look at Christ's life. He possessed great fire and strength when he threw the money changers out of the temple in Jerusalem. He did not say, "Please, Mr. Money Changers, kindly get out of my Father's house." No, he physically threw them out. The Vedic[1] definition of a man of God is one who is softer than the flowers where kindness is concerned and stronger than the thunder where principles are at stake. Many people feel that to be spiritual is to give up the body and ignore it, but that is a false concept. The ideal is to become master of the body so it can be used as a tool for Spirit. We need to be rooted in our hands and feet and body to accomplish the work and know the glory of Spirit. Many saints have spent a part of their lives in solitude to become one with the Divine Essence, but once they became anchored in God the pattern is always the same—service, service, service; fulfilling the Will of God, working in tune with the Red Ray. Saint Francis, Saint Teresa of Avila, Saint Ignatius—all are examples of lives given to Divine service. The spiritual life is one of balance—it is meditation on God, along with service to God and mankind. Many people work for a while and then tire, but saints have unlimited physical energy. Feeling the power of God behind them, they become so saturated with energy that many of them did not even feel the need to sleep.

Mother Teresa of Calcutta is a good example of one who has centered in the Red Ray and brought her love to the people—love in action. A lot of physical energy and vitality is needed to carry on the work of serving and feeding the poor and destitute of India. The work of her Sisters of Charity is one of intense physical activity and labor. From early morning to late at night they unselfishly bring God's Love to all.

Whenever we want to accomplish noble desires, we can visualize and concentrate on the Red Ray of strength and vitality, until we become charged with its vitalizing energy and powers.

THE ORANGE LEVEL OF CONSCIOUSNESS

The Orange Ray symbolizes optimism, self-confidence, enthusiasm and courage. It is also the social ray of service to mankind. Manifested it brings great courage and enthusiasm in working and mingling with people to bring about positive changes on this planet.[2] During his incarnation on earth Krishna[3] lived amongst the people. He served and socialized bringing God to all. As he played his flute, he awakened the longing for and Love of God in men's hearts. People came to him and he certainly did not push them away; he embraced them. His love for humanity was so great that he promised that whenever there is a decline of righteousness and a rise of unrighteousness, he would incarnate again on this earth to protect the good and to destroy evil. This is how he manifested the Orange Ray.

During the famous battle between the Pandavas and Kauravas on the battlefield of Kurukshetra as portrayed in the Bhagavad-Gita, Krishna instructed his beloved devotee Arjuna[4] to perform his dharma (duty). He encouraged him to perform his duty for God with confidence and courage, being non-attached to the fruits of actions. He counseled Arjuna that everyone, depending on his station in life, has certain dharma to perform. "You are a warrior and your dharma is to fight for a righteous cause."[5] He taught that performance of one's duties for God without a self-motive or attachment to the fruits of action brings liberation. It is not non-action and renunciation of our duties that brings liberation, but performance of them with enthusiastic confidence and courage for God alone. Arjuna's duty as a warrior was to do battle with his relatives to regain the lost kingdom of the Pandavas. With Krishna's guidance he fought the battle with the Orange Ray of confidence and courage and was victorious.

We need to manifest great self-confidence—which is the natural state of the soul—when we do battle with our egos or lower selves in meditation. We will benefit if we adopt positive attitudes of enthusiasm as we overcome our restless natures and concentrate single-pointedly on God. When we inwardly feel what our true duty in life is and are convinced that it is the Will of God for us, we can then bring together all our attributes in confidence and manifest them in our lives. Arjuna did not want to fight, but once he realized that this was what God expected of him he showed great confidence and enthusiasm in battle.

Mahatma Gandhi,[6] in manifesting his doctrine of non-violence, showed great confidence. He stated that his doctrine was not for cowards but for those who had confidence and strength. Gandhi's deeply-held religious and political convictions often caused him to be the victim of violence, but he would never fight to defend his body. When he smiled the ever widening gaps between his teeth bore testimony to the one-sided skirmishes. He was often kicked and beaten until he lapsed into unconsciousness. Still he continued his fight for needed reforms. The injustice of the Hindu caste system and prevailing political prejudices caused him to work with ever-increasing fervor until India achieved its independence and the caste system was abolished. We can learn much from this great man of truth and fearless strength and courage. Many martyrs have laid down their lives for the glory of God and truth with confidence and soul strength. Let us remember to call on the Orange Ray to manifest in our lives when we need enthusiastic confidence to serve our brothers and sisters in need.

More and more group consciousness is emerging and in the future it will be a basic life style everywhere. The social service aspect of the Orange Ray will be the essence of new age communities if they function on spiritual principles. People within these communities and those who come in contact with them will have a divine opportunity to learn of the power of the Orange Ray.

THE YELLOW LEVEL OF CONSCIOUSNESS

The Yellow Ray symbolizes mental or intellectual power, happiness and joy. The Yellow Ray gives us the ability to delve deeply into a problem and come up with the right solution. Our society is largely geared toward developing the intellectual aspect of this ray. It is very much a part of our educational system to the exclusion of almost everything else. In order for education to be of optimum benefit it must also stimulate the other Cosmic Color Rays as well. The Golden

Yellow Ray helps us to tune in with the wisdom of the cosmos and is often called the Christ Ray. There is a vast difference between the powers of mind Christ possessed and the limited intellect we know. Even the greatest scientist uses only a fraction of his infinite potential.

Shankara,[7] reorganizer of the ancient monastic order of swamis in India, manifested the power of Jana Yoga[8] or Divine Wisdom. When Shankara was only three he was familiar with the Puranas and could read the deepest philosophy with understanding. When he was twelve he wrote his famous commentary on the Brahma-Sutras, the essence of the Upanishads. This reminds one of Christ, who at twelve was about his Father's business and amazed the scribes in Jerusalem with his profound understanding. Shankara was unique among the outstanding spiritual teachers of the world in that he was a great scholar and left many written works behind him. He had one of the keenest minds of all times.

There are many interesting stories centering around Shankara and his favorite disciple Padmapada "Lotus-foot." The disciple received this name after a miraculous experience with his guru.[9] Upon hearing the voice of his guru calling him from the opposite shores of a river he jumped into the water without hesitation. Shankara caused the lotus flowers lying under water to emerge and support the footsteps of his disciple as he moved across the rushing water. On another occasion Padmapada accidentally burnt a commentary on the Brahma-Sutras he had written. Shankara had read his work once and to the disciple's joy recited it accurately from memory while he again wrote it down. Such is the power and magnitude of mind waiting to be discovered by all children of God. Whenever we are working on a problem we would benefit by cultivating a feeling that we are saturated with the power of the Yellow Ray, that all the power of Spirit is with us.

Let us search into the heart of Joy. It is said that a saint that is sad is a sad saint.[10] A saint that is happy and content has truly found God. All saints of India have expressed indescribable joy and ecstatic raptures in their devotional bakti[11] or chanting to God in the form of Divine Mother.[12] Saint Francis felt the same joy and he and his brothers would often sing most of the night away in their praises to God. Their lives were one of divine merriment as if they were lost and drunk in the Joy of God.

I personally have found it very difficult to think of and concentrate on the suffering of Christ, for my heart and soul have always felt the need to approach Him as the Lord of Joy. I often reflected that no one painted Christ with a smile. This sternness was certainly not the Christ I felt I had tuned in to. For several weeks I prayed that He might show himself to me with a smile on His lips. The answer to my prayers came about a month later as I was riding my bicycle in a desert in California. As I pedaled, my eyes turned to see a statue in a church off in the distance. I asked my companions if they would like to go and see the statue and we all went. I felt compelled to see that statue. When we arrived I could not believe what I saw. It was a statue of Christ and He was sitting in meditation with a glorious smile on His face! Since that day no one can convince me that Christ is not the Lord of Joy—a perfect manifestation of the Yellow Ray—and that He is trying to encourage us all to approach Him and become one with Him in joy. If you ever feel depressed, visualize the Yellow Ray to help you and bathe you in its Light. Feel the special vibration of its optimistic, sorrow-banishing joy.

THE GREEN LEVEL OF CONSCIOUSNESS

The Green Ray symbolizes balance, harmony, peacemaking, brotherhood, hope, growth, healing and love. Green is the ray of the heart and when the heart is completely open to

Divine Mother, then Her wondrous love flows through our consciousness to all. In order to love Divine Mother with all the green level of awareness, we need to give Her every ounce of our love. When we love Divine Mother so completely, we will behold Her manifested in everyone, and only by loving the Mother in all can we then truly say that we love our neighbors as ourselves. Spirit can manifest Itself in any form. The Divine Mother aspect of God often appears to those devotees who seek infinite compassion and unconditional love. Many saints of India have attained liberation through their single-pointed love for the all forgiving Divine Mother.

Saint Francis' love for Christ was so intense that the magnetism of his love drew Christ to him every evening when they communed in intimacy, "as a friend speaketh unto a friend." He so loved his beloved Christ that he even wanted to share the suffering of his Lord so that he might be more one with Him. He bore the wounds of Christ as an example of his love. His love extended to everyone—brother sun, sister moon and to all of God's creatures. Filled with the ecstatic Joy of God, he was able to see the beauty in all things, the majesty of the trees and the delicate splendor of a wayside flower. He experienced the tender love that God showers on His creation. Conscious of the oneness permeating all things through their common Creator, he beheld everything and everyone as brothers and sisters.

This intense, encompassing feeling of brotherhood and harmony was cradled in Saint Francis's heart. He felt the same love for the earth, sky, leaf, flower, beast and man—for everything under the sun. His sensitive heart was not less concerned about the wellbeing of a bee, the fate of a flower or a bird than about the affairs of his newly-formed order. He communicated with the same heartfelt intensity of love to animals, bushes, crops, mountains, to the wind and clouds, to earth, water, fire, and air and encouraged them all to praise and love God and thank Him for His special gift of life. He even felt embracing love for brother rat who ran over his chest when he lay dying in his hut.

The Green Ray is the healing ray, and the energy of God manifested itself through this saint to others. He healed people of blindness and other maladies, and his sympathetic and compassionate heart comforted those in the leprosy colonies. Great masters of all religions have had the gift of healing and channeled the divine essence to relieve the suffering of mankind. Krishna, Buddha, Christ, Babaji, Yogananda, Kabir, Ramakrishna all were pure channels of God's glory and grace—the Green Ray manifested.

At the moment of death Mahatma Gandhi, like Christ, showed his love for mankind in a spirit of peace and harmony. As an assassin's bullet entered his small, frail body, he reverently raised his hands with palms together in the ancient Hindu symbol of greeting, silently and lovingly bestowing his forgiveness in this final gesture. Christ, in the last hour, worked his mightiest miracle of love for mankind when he prayed to God and said, "Father forgive them, for they know not what they do."[13-14] Whenever we especially need the quality of peace and harmony with our brothers and sisters—and we always do—let us call on the power of the Green Ray that we may bring heaven on earth.

THE BLUE LEVEL OF CONSCIOUSNESS

The Blue Ray symbolizes inspiration, creativity, spiritual understanding, faith and devotion. Moses' faith and trust in God so moved him as he communed with his Creator on Mount Horeb, that he challenged the power of the Pharaoh in Egypt for the release of his people. His faith in the Divine Mercy of God allowed him to predict the ten plagues and to stretch his rod over the Red Sea and call forth power over the elements.

Through his communion he understood the ways of God and the ten commandments were as second nature to him. What no one else noted, he perceived; what no one else understood, he understood. He knew whatever God spoke would come to pass and it was not difficult for him to keep faith, for he communed with God as a friend speaketh unto a friend. When everyone feared God, he knew Him as a friend and could talk to Him as an understanding and loving Father. He was able to talk to God as a dear son would who pleaded time and time again for the ignorance and grossness of his people, that they might be forgiven for their baseness and sins. Through the time of wandering through the desert for forty years he showed his faith and devotion to God. When all others doubted, he held firm in his devotion and trust.

Sri Chaitanya's[15] devotion to Lord Krishna filled him with reverent devotion for the Lord of the Universe. Chaitanya preached and practiced pure bhakti (love for God) and instilled in whomever he met the love and desire for Krishna. As he traveled he sang the praises of God, and people were caught up in his devotional chanting. The vibration of love in his songs of praise often cleared the debris of ignorance that separated souls from Spirit. In his presence the melody of praise opened the doors of people's souls, and they glimpsed the divine indwelling presence. As he sang he often swooned in ecstatic trance at the name of Krishna and would be absorbed in the deepest rapture. Even as an infant the name of God was in his heart. When he was a baby in his mother's arms he wept unceasingly, but when his mother and the neighboring woman would cry out "Haribol," which means "God," he would stop crying. As a result the name of God in the utterance of "Haribol" continually resounded in the baby Chaitanya's home.

Every saint manifests divine creativity even in the tiniest endeavors. Saint Thérèsa of Lisieux was known as the little flower, the saint of little things. She would perform little tasks in devotional creativity to her Lord. The Divine will accept even the tiniest straw, if it is offered to Him in a devotional attitude of love. The greatest masterpieces are those that are divinely inspired, and the creativity that went into manifesting them is often beyond comprehension. We can learn to tune in with the Blue Ray through deep meditation. If we do this we will realize that it has a guiding intelligence within its vibration, and that we can lovingly call on this vibration and ask it to work its devotional creative power through us.

THE INDIGO LEVEL OF CONSCIOUSNESS

The Indigo Ray symbolizes spiritual perception and intuition. There are countless people who have had hunches and visions and the messages have often been profound. The mind of Spirit is pure intuition. It knows and It does not have to intellectualize about anything, for in God's consciousness there is no time, no past, present or future; only the eternal now. When one is in tune with Spirit, one knows all by intuition. Cosmic Consciousness[16] means having the entire knowledge of the universe in one's consciousness—for one's consciousness is, in essence, the universe. To know everything instantaneously is the power of complete unfoldment of intuition—the Indigo Ray.

The quickest way to open up the power of intuition is to gaze at a point between the eyebrows (the spiritual eye) and uplift and concentrate one's energy at this sacred center. The more the spiritual eye is opened, the greater will be the power of intuition. Mankind in general only operates through the five senses and the sixth sense is undeveloped and forgotten. By meditation, stilling the restless, sense-distracted mind and holding the attention at the spiritual eye, intuition will spontaneously awaken. When the mind is calm, it gains the capacity to mirror the universe in its wholeness. Instead of seeing everything in creation as separate pieces of a cosmic puzzle, the mind reflects the whole picture in its entirety.[17]

The greatest trap in the spiritual life is pride. Some people who get a couple of flashes of knowledge and some spiritual experiences feel they have to be leaders and convert the world. Sometimes a little knowledge is a very dangerous thing. A bottle that is filled with water when shaken makes very little noise but when it is only partially full it makes a lot of noise. And so it is with some people who have a little experience. Their ego loudly resounds I, me and mine, always bringing the conversation back to themselves. We need to be humble and realize how far we have to go on the road to perfection and always be mindful that we spend our time wisely, changing ourselves instead of trying to change others.

A brother in a monastic order was so cautious about this point that he went to the opposite extreme. He had received the gift that whenever he spoke of God people would be moved. He was so fearful of being drowned in prideful thoughts that he asked his brothers to whip him after every service he gave. This method is drastic and encourages negativity, but the point is clear. We are all potential saints and that is where spiritual pride may be a pitfall. He who has truly become saintly does not know that he is a saint. He is just concerned with loving God and doing God's work in this world.

Mohammed's[18] intuition[19] was awakened as he meditated in a small cave on Mount Hira just outside Mecca. The angel Gabriel appeared to him and told him that he was the messenger of the one God and that he must spread the idea of one God. Mohammed had from an early age felt inwardly that the belief of the Christians and Jews that there was only one God was correct. As time passed, this understanding grew in his heart and he was convinced that the one God was not only for the Christians and Jews but that He was the common Father of all peoples, of all creation. In the beginning his mission moved slowly, so Gabriel appeared once again to him as he meditated in his cave at Mount Hira and commanded him to go out and preach to the world. His intuition was so keen that he saw the folly in worshipping the idols at Kaaba—the holy shrine of the Arab world. He called these idols senseless blocks of stone. In meditation the truths of God and creation were revealed to him, as was his mission and purpose on earth. He intuitively saw the plan of his work and carried it out with divine enthusiasm and confidence.

Guru Nanak,[20] leader of the Sikhs, also felt from his contemplation that there was only one God, and the differences and prejudices between men were nonsense. As a youth he could not understand why he could not play with a neighbor's boy because he was of a lower caste and considered unclean. While he meditated intensely for three days, the town folk thought he had died, since they could not find him anywhere. They saw his clothes by the bank of a river and thought he had drowned. Divine intuitive realizations were granted to him during this time and when he went back to town he could not speak when questioned. Finally after some time he simply said "There is no Hindu. There is no Muslim."

He came to realize that both Hindus and Muslims believed in the same God, and the only difference was that they said the same things in different ways. He understood that it was because of these differences that there was so much hatred, misery, and unhappiness; that they were the cause of needless wars. He began his mission by wearing half of his clothes from the holy robes of the Hindus and the other half from the Muslims. He taught that we should all look upon God as our one Father and see each other as brothers and sisters.[21] In time both Muslims and Hindus considered him their divine leader.

While he was dying Nanak asked his disciples to pray for him and felt a tension after some time of silence. He found that the reason for the disturbance was that both sides were bickering about what should be done with his body. The Muslims wanted to bury him according to their custom, while the Hindus wanted to cremate him according to theirs. Guru Nanak counselled them to put flowers on either side of him, Hindus on his right and Muslims on his left. Those whose flowers remained fresh in the morning could do with his body as they wished. Guru Nanak died in the night and in the morning both sets of flowers remained fresh and vibrant. Both Mohammed and Guru Nanak had realized through their meditative, awakened intuition that there is only one God, the Lord of all creation. They both followed their inner intuitive guidance to fulfill their missions of brotherhood, teaching that we are all equal in the eyes of God.

THE VIOLET LEVEL OF CONSCIOUSNESS

The Cosmic Violet Ray symbolizes divine realization, humility, and creative imagination. When we look on the Violet Ray, spiritual perceptions are felt for longer periods of time, as consciousness retires closer to the center of the soul in the thousand-petaled lotus in the brain. In ever-deepening meditation, the presence of God awakens as Ever New Joy in our souls. The true depth and beauty of God is revealed to us. He is unfathomable. He has no beginning or end. He is spaceless, unconfined, everlasting, complete—the one indivisible being. He is the root of all love and power, the origin of all knowledge. All creation is His body, all intelligence is His mind, and all love is His heart. He is the only real substance—the all in all. Nothing is outside of Him. He is everything. He is the ocean and the waves of creation. He is eternally aware of Himself and everything within Himself. He knows the play of every electron at each moment in time and follows that electron for eternity until it realizes its oneness in Him. He is love, joy, the moon and the stars. He exists and is all that exists.

Creative imagination and the power of visualization give the devotee of truth the power to materialize whatever he desires at will. In tune with the laws of God, dwelling in the three planes of existence, one is able to manifest all the so-called miracles that have been performed by the saints of all religions. Nothing can be considered a miracle, for everything works in accordance with God's physical or spiritual laws. It is because man is ignorant of many of the laws of Spirit, that he cannot explain or understand certain phenomena. He that is close to the bosom of Spirit can create worlds even as God does.

Babaji[22] materialized a palace in the Himalayan mountains for his beloved disciple Lahiri Mahasaya. Through the power of his thought he visualized the picture of the palace in his mind, then materialized the palace into physical reality. By gathering the atoms together with the power of his will, he arranged them into the material shape of a palace, which in every way was real to the five senses of taste, touch, smell, sight and hearing. Through this divine display of creative strength he was able to work out the last desire locked in his beloved disciple's heart.

When Lahiri Mahasaya experienced the divine gift of the palace his heart was satisfied and he was freed from all desires and all karma.[23] There were no chains holding him to the physical plane of existence any longer. As soon as he attained this freedom, Babaji dematerialized the palace by removing his will which had held the atoms of the palace together. As God could annihilate this universe in an instant by removing His Will, so Babaji dematerialized the palace he had created by withdrawing his. The atoms that structured the palace were no longer maintained by Babaji's will and so they returned to the pool of atomic energy.

Christ changed water into wine at the marriage feast and also fed five thousand men, women and children with five loaves of bread and two small fishes. The power of the mind is inexhaustible when one is in tune with the supreme laws of God. It is by discipline that we may learn to master ourselves and so be able to work in tune with God's Cosmic Laws.

An interesting story centers around Paramahansa Yogananda, founder of Self-Realization Fellowship. His mission was to show the basic oneness between the original Christianity as taught by Lord Jesus and the original Yoga as taught by Lord Krishna. His mission was also to bring the highly advanced scientific technique of Kriya Yoga to the west. This technique enables one to have direct personal experience of God within, through one's own effort in meditation. Yogananda and his devotees were visiting their retreat center in Encinitas, California. Everyone was thirsty after the trip, but the devotees could find only a pint of carrot juice in the refrigerator. The master asked them to bring the juice and six eight ounce glasses, one for each devotee. Yogananda took the juice and filled each glass to the brim. All the devotees were amazed as they drank and their thirst was satisfied in more ways than one.

The quality closest to God's heart is humility. He who is humble does not know he is humble. Sri Ramakrishna[24] worshipped God in the form of Kali (Divine Mother) at the temple at Dakshineswar. She is the Universal Mother, "my Mother," as Ramakrishna would say, the All-powerful, who reveals Herself to Her children under different aspects and Divine Incarnations; the Visible God who leads the elect to the Invisible Reality; and if it so pleases Her, She takes away the last trace of ego from a created being and merges it in the Absolute, the undifferentiated God. Through Her grace the finite ego loses itself in the illimitable ego—Atman-Brahma. As he continued to concentrate on the Divine Mother, she did help him to remove the last traces of ego. He felt himself to be a child of the Divine Mother. He learned to surrender himself completely to Her will and let Her direct him. "O Mother," he would constantly pray, "I have taken refuge in Thee. Teach me what to do and what to say. Thy will is paramount everywhere and is for the good of Thy children. Merge my will in Thy will and make me Thy instrument."

Bhagavan Krishna's life was unique in that he was a great prophet, yet he cheerfully and conscientiously carried out his duties as a king. He practiced a balanced life of meditation and activity being both a monarch and a saviour of mankind. Despite his wealth, power and fame, Krishna remained ever humble. It is said that Saint Bhrigu was intent on finding the most humble of prophets so that he could become his disciple and be initiated by him. He sought long and hard, traveling throughout the three planes of creation—physical, astral, and causal realms—in his search for his guru. He tested many divine personages and always found some flaw in their practice of humility.

He was becoming discouraged because he could not find anyone who had blossomed and manifested the sweetness of this sacred quality. When Bhrigu was seeking on the physical plane he decided to test Bhagavan Krishna, whom he found asleep. Bhrigu immediately started kicking Krishna in the chest and shouted, "You sleeping fool, wake up and see who is present here." Krishna awakened in a state of divine tranquility and evenmindedness. A sincere and loving smile was playing on his lips. Krishna asked Saint Bhrigu if his foot was hurt as he tenderly massaged the kicking foot. Bhrigu was beside himself with remorse for kicking such a great one, but at the same time he was filled with ecstatic joy. He realized he had found him—the humble one. He danced and exclaimed that he had found the most humble incarnation of God, who was indeed one with the humble Lord of the Universe Himself. Bhrigu realized Krishna alone could teach him to know the humble God of Creation and he became Krishna's disciple.

THE WHITE LIGHT OF SPIRIT

The White Light of Spirit symbolizes the sum total of all the Cosmic Rays. It is the awareness of the soul's oneness with God, the complete fulfillment of love. "Thou shalt love the Lord thy God with all thy heart, soul, mind and strength and thy neighbor as thyself."[25] Loving God with all thy heart and thy neighbor as thyself is a complete manifestation of the Green Ray. It encompasses the Blue Devotional Ray as well. To love God with all one's soul is the fulfillment of the Indigo and Violet Rays. To love God with all one's mind is the complete fulfillment of the Yellow Ray of awareness. To love God with all one's strength is the Orange and Red Ray implemented, uplifting one's energy Godward. When we learn to love God completely with heart, soul, mind, and strength, we will perceive and become one with the White Light of Spirit.

Saint Teresa of Avila was one of the greatest of the mystics —the saint of ecstasy. On many occasions the Lord would come and suspend her soul, and her breath would stop. During these raptures she would be withdrawn into the mansion of her soul. She traveled to the innermost court of her interior castle and merged in oneness with the Lord of the Universe. She found the wave of her life merging into the ocean of Spirit. She realized the ultimate truth that we are souls made in the Image of God. What He is we are, and this is the innate nature of everyone.

Lord Buddha experienced the supreme state of Buddhahood under the Bodhi Tree, as he meditated long and deeply on ultimate reality. He vowed not to move until he realized truth, and his determination and persistence allowed him to attain the ultimate goal for which he strove. Overcoming all lures of temptation, he became bathed in the White Light of God and was no longer Siddhartha, but became Buddha the Enlightened One. Buddha then taught his doctrine of desirelessness.

He said that all suffering, pain, fear and hatred come from desire. The man who is free from desire need not worry—whom indeed has he to fear?

Buddha's doctrine was that Nirvana was not a state of negation or nothingness, but that by overcoming desire we can overcome our restless minds and hearts that prevent us from seeing our oneness with God. God is the universe—we are the universe—Thou Art That. "Know ye not that ye are the Temple of God and that the Spirit of God dwelleth in you?"[26] Being one with God means being omniscient, omnipresent. We may behold everything simultaneously—a blade of grass, the moon and stars.

Christ, who fasted forty days and nights in the wilderness, received the same enlightenment as Buddha. He, too, was tested by Satan and conquered and realized his oneness with God in the solitude of meditation. Jesus merged his consciousness into the Christ Consciousness, the supreme intelligence in every atom of creation, as Buddha and Krishna had done before him. They all arrived at the same point of consciousness, but each maintained his own individuality. Christ Consciousness, Buddhahood and Krishna Consciousness all are the same thing. All liberated masters uplifted their consciousness from the body to merge in the universal intelligence and become true Sons of God. We can all achieve this state of divine realization if we learn to expand our consciousness in meditation and become Christlike, Buddhalike, Krishnalike. "As many as received Him, to them gave He power to become the Sons of God."[27]

We are all Sons of God. No man can come unto the Father except he receives and merges his consciousness in the Christ Consciousness state as Jesus himself did. When we become one with this state of consciousness we will realize that Christ, Buddha, Krishna—in fact everyone—is a Son of God, special and unique in the eyes of the Father.

Paramahansa Yogananda received this blessed state in June 1948 when he entered his great samadhi.[28] From that day until his conscious exit from the body in 1952 he was constantly one with God in nirbakalpa samadhi. His consciousness was simultaneously one with the ocean of God and the waves of creation and he had full awareness of this state day and night. As he sat in his chair at the Self-Realization Center, he suddenly entered the divine trance. The devotees around him heard the Divine Mother Herself speaking through his lips to them. Yogananda kept telling the Divine Mother that she was taking him too fast, and he kept repeating over and over for hours "You, You, You."

Every saint of every religion has fully perfected himself in his divine nature. No matter what prophet you look at, the message is the same—will you not follow our example and perfect yourself and find out who you really are—not what you intellectually think you are? Different masters emphasize certain truths and messages for the needs of a particular group of people at a certain time. If you honestly look at all the masters with the eyes of understanding, you will discover their oneness. The positive qualities of certain color rays need to be emphasized at times in order to help overcome the opposite, negative qualities that mankind are indulging in. God in His kindness has sent countless messengers of truth to help in our evolution. Let us all work to follow the example of the great ones, for we can be perfected and realize our oneness with God in this life if we will make the effort.

Notes—Chapter 3

1. Vedas: The four scriptural texts of the Hindus: Rig Veda, Sama Veda, Yajur Veda and Atharva Veda.

2. "Whatever ye put out as usury to increase it with the substance of others shall have no increase from God; but whatever ye shall give in alms, as seeking the face of God, shall be doubled to you." Koran

3. Krishna: A king and sage of India who achieved God realization three thousand years before Christ. His divine counsel is written in the Bhagavad-Gita.

4. Arjuna: The beloved and exalted disciple of Bhagavan Krishna. The transforming message of the Bhagavad-Gita was given to Arjuna by Krishna around 3,000 B.C.

5. "Surrender not to unmanliness. It is unbecoming of thee. O scorcher of foes, forsake this small weak-heartedness and arise!" Bhagavad-Gita VI:26

6. Gandhi, Mohandas K. ("Mahatma"): India's political saint who taught the doctrine of nonviolence and won India's independence in 1947 without war.

7. Shankara, Swami: An Indian philosopher and master who is thought to have lived in the ninth century A.D. He taught that God is not a negative abstraction but that He is ever-conscious, ever-existing, ever-new Bliss.

8. Jana Yoga: Yoga signifies union of the soul with Spirit. Jana means wisdom; therefore, it is union with God through wisdom.

9. Guru: A God-realized master who has been appointed by God to lead others to realize their oneness in Spirit.

10. St. Francis de Sales

11. Bhakti Yoga: Yoga signifies union of the soul with Spirit. Bhakti means love; therefore, it is union with God through all-surrendering love.

12. Divine Mother: The Hindu scriptures state that God is both personal and impersonal, immanent and transcendent. Many Hindu saints have found salvation by seeking God through the personal aspect of the Divine Mother. She is the embodiment of unconditional love and compassion.

13. Luke 23:34

14. "By the accident of fortune a man may rule the world for a time, by the virtue of love he may rule the world forever." Lao-Tzu

15. Chaitanya: Born in India on Feb. 18, 1486. He was a great pandit and attained liberation through his devotional chanting to God.

16. Cosmic Consciousness: The Supreme Intelligence existing beyond creation. It is also the highest meditative state, the one in which there is the realization of oneness with God both in and beyond vibratory creation.

17. "Make peace with yourself and heaven and earth will make peace with you. Endeavor to enter your own cell, and you will see the heavens; because the one and the other are one and the same, and when you enter one you see the two." St. Isaak of Syria

18. Mohammed: Seventh-century sage; the founder of Islam.

19. Intuition: The "sixth sense" or the all-knowing quality of the soul, which directly perceives truth without using the instruments of the senses or of reason.

20. Nanak: The illumined medieval prophet of the Sikhs in India.

21. "Let not a man glory in this, that he love his country; let him rather glory in this, that he love his kind." Persian Proverb

22. Babaji: The deathless master who lives in the Himalayas beyond public view. His God-given mission is to assist all prophets in all lands through time immemorial to carry out their special dispensations and uplift the planet to God Consciousness.

23. Karma: the mathematical justice of the universe. Mankind reaps what it sows and is thus subject to the effects of its past actions. Mankind is a molder of its own destiny through its own thoughts and deeds. Whatever is put out will inevitability be returned.

24. Ramakrishna: Born in India on Feb. 18, 1836. He realized oneness with God through his devotion to Spirit in the form of Divine Mother.

25. Luke 10:27

26. I Corinthians 3:16

27. John 1:12

28. Samadhi: A state of meditation in which the devotee realizes his oneness with the object of his concentration—God.

4

Overcoming Psychological Problems with the Divine Rays

TREATING PSYCHOLOGICAL PROBLEMS THROUGH THE COLOR RAYS

A PSYCHOLOGICAL PROBLEM, if nurtured and allowed to grow, will manifest in the body and eventually cause serious physical problems. These inharmonies also manifest as dirty muddy colors and dark spots in the aura. The petals of the different chakra centers are indicative of energy rays that flow into the body to maintain and help the functioning of the various organs and systems in the body. By treating the chakras, the entire body can be stimulated. Not only do the different rays of the chakras have physical qualities; they have psychological and emotional properties as well.

If the negative aspect of a ray is manifesting, it will show up in the physical body. By understanding what emotions are locked in different body parts and the emotional and the psychological qualities of these, we can activate the chakra centers to bring about physical, mental, and emotional harmony and healing. When the undistorted Cosmic Rays are allowed to flow unobstructed into consciousness, then perfection is experienced in every level of being. The mission of life is to remove all blocks that have been created, so the Light of God may

36

enter and transform a person into His likeness. In healing different psychological and emotional problems, it is very beneficial to use the white light along with color meditation combined with breathing exercise. (See methods of treatment section).

In order to be cured, it is important for persons to get in touch with themselves so that there can be a release of all anxieties and drama held in the body. When the realization dawns that a situation experienced and not dealt with in the past or present is bringing on the problem, then the healing can be effective. In discovering the root source of the problem one can then transform it with a new program and pattern of thinking and acting. Meditation, positive affirmations and color therapy can and will help in reprogramming the subconscious and conscious minds to create positive attitudes and actions to overcome all physical, mental and spiritual inharmonies.

THE RED RAY
(Coccygeal Center)

The vitalizing and stimulating power of the Red Ray will help in overcoming feelings of inertia, depression, fear, and melancholy. It is also a great aid to those who are afraid of life and are inclined to turn their backs on the world or feel like escaping. The Red Ray helps plant one's feet firmly on the earth. If a person is too spaced out—always living in the future—the Red Ray will help to root that person in the now. It supplies the energy and physical motivation to help reach for and accomplish one's goals in life.

If there is a predominance of dirty shades of red in the aura, there is a need to work on overcoming the lower passions and desires. The dark, cloudy shades are degenerating and sinister and are indicative of one who is living to satisfy the sense appetites. Such a person finds that life bounces him around like a rubber ball as he fluctuates from one desire to the next. Hatred, anger, selfishness, greed, cruelty, perhaps a bullying nature, overimpulsiveness, and reactive tendencies are all negative qualities that manifest when the pure Cosmic Ray of Red has been obstructed.[1]

Anger, when used consciously as righteous indignation, emits a brilliant, scarlet flame. Many emotions can be used negatively or positively depending on one's state of consciousness. If at will one chooses to manifest anger because he can see that the emotion will serve him or others, then pure vibrant colors will manifest in the aura. When emotions are used this way a person will be a master and not a slave of emotions and circumstances in his life. Mankind is free to choose whatever emotions he wishes to manifest. If one feels he has no choice and automatically responds to certain issues, then he has formed a deep habit and needs to work to become master of his responses once again.

Meditate on receiving the full power of the Red Cosmic Beam that its strength and vitality may enrich your life. As we meditate and the Cosmic Ray manifests clearly and brightly in the aura, then we will begin to show the qualities of affection, generosity, sensitivity to others, ambition to better one's self and strong physical propensities. Rather than jumping from one stimulus to the next, we will be able to think before we act and harness our newly-acquired vitality to carry each project to completion. Instead of expending our energy in conquering and dominating others, we will be able to use this energy to conquer undesirable qualities within ourselves.

THE ORANGE RAY
(Sacral Center)

If the Orange Ray is obstructed and not allowed to flow properly in consciousness, insensitivity to others can manifest.

If the perfect essence of the Orange Ray is visualized entering the sacral center and saturating one's whole self, then a sensitivity and respect for others will come into being. The right attitude is very important in the healing process. If, for example, a person concentrates on the thought that all of creation is an extension of one's self then the power of the Orange Ray meditation will be heightened. By feeling the Orange Ray and perceiving the holiness of all things, a divine sensitivity will shine forth.

The tendency to believe too readily without any weighing, skepticism or discrimination can be ameliorated by the vibration of the Orange Ray. People inclined this way are usually mentally lazy or credulous and easily convinced. When meditating on the Orange Ray it is helpful to keep in mind the words of Lord Buddha. "Believe nothing because it is traditional, or because you yourselves have imagined it. Do not believe what your teacher tells you merely out of respect for the teacher. But whatsoever, after due examination and analysis, you find to be conducive to the good, the benefit, the welfare of all beings—that doctrine believe and cling to, take it as your guide." By fostering the inner discriminative capacities, a person can determine his true goals which bring satisfaction and happiness.

Suspicion is an emotion that is held in the abdominal region and treatments with the Orange Ray is beneficial. By bringing in Orange through the sacral center and saturating the abdominal region, this emotion can be released. Suspicion is a manifestation of insecurity and lack of trust. Condemnation of the faults of others acts like a magnet that draws those qualities to one's being. In time that quality will begin to manifest. Concentration on the good qualities of others will stimulate positive attributes within oneself.

A destructive and cruel nature can be treated with the Orange Ray. Through meditation on Orange negative emotions may be transformed into their opposite, positive attributes which are constructiveness and pity.[2] Racial prejudice can also be replaced by this vibration. The social Orange Ray can help humanity realize we are all brothers and sisters with one common parent: God.

If the orange of the aura is muddy, then the qualities of selfish pride and indulgence in power-seeking and manipulative behavior patterns may manifest. One may become superficial in actions in an effort to "make it" in society so that acceptance and a good reputation may be enjoyed. Instead of using underhanded tactics to climb the social ladder, a person may turn to the opposite extreme and be anti-social, finding he is fed up with all the games people play.

Meditate on the pure Orange Ray so that the divine nature of an optimistic, hospitable, humanitarianism may warm your consciousness. When the Orange has saturated your being, you will be warm and welcoming to others and will love to work for their benefit. Through pure Orange we can expand our consciousness and see all of humanity as brothers and sisters and realize that we are all one big family.

THE YELLOW RAY
(Lumbar or Solar Plexus Center)

Often when someone is fearful he feels as if his stomach is going to turn over. In some cases the feeling is so intense that it manifests in diarrhea. Many times the situation develops into a perpetually nervous stomach. Through various incarnations, a tremendous amount of fear may have been locked into the solar plexus region. Oftentimes a person cannot understand why he is fearful, but as soon as certain situations present themselves fear appears for no apparent reason. There are many different fears—fear of public speaking, fear of water, fear of the dark, fear of losing a loved one. In some cases this fear has been established by some incident that happened in a past life that caused a great deal of humiliation, anguish or even death. Throughout various incarnations this fear may have built up until it is completely distorted and out of control. As soon as some threatening circumstance approaches, a person may automatically feel fear welling up inside. Fear can be overcome through Divine Wisdom, if you realize that as a child of God nothing can hurt your soul.[3]

If the problem is chronic and deeply rooted, then meditation on the Yellow Ray will aid in rebuilding the nervous system and gradually release the tension from the fearful experiences from the solar plexus. By coming in touch with the original cause of fear a person can gain understanding and learn the wisdom to remove it. Feel that the solar plexus is bathed in yellow light. Feel that the negative thoughts and the whole situation are encompassed in yellow light and see all fear melting into this brilliant yellow. Meditate on the color orange and feel that the quality of courage is rebuilding and inspiring you. The soul is fearless, a divine manifestation of courage. Shame, treachery, aversion, anger, jealousy, ignorance, desire, worldliness, avarice, despondency, despair are all problems that can be released through treatment via the lumbar center with yellow.

When a dirty muddy yellow is found in an aura, it is an indication that a person tends to be mentally and verbally aggressive with an overly critical and picky nature. This judgmental attitude causes one to become very egotistical and separates that person from others. A pale yellow in the aura indicates a gentle, soft, intellectual, but not very vigorous disposition. With the lighter shades nervous conditions may manifest.

Meditate on the pure yellow beam of the Cosmic Ray that its great intellectual and mental power may rule our consciousnesses. When the pure radiance of the Yellow Ray shines in our auras, we will find that we are highly creative and have great precision and analytical abilities. We will find that we have become flexible and adaptable to change. We will also manifest efficiency in planning and organizational work. When we are in tune with the Yellow Ray, no problem will remain unsolved under the scalpel of our intellects. We will also learn that it is better to work to change ourselves rather than others and it will become clear to us that we must balance our heads with our hearts.

THE GREEN RAY
(Dorsal or Heart Center)

Visualizing the Green Ray saturating the heart is very beneficial for any deep-rooted feeling of regret. A helpful attitude when working on this psychological problem is to learn from the past, but not to dwell there instead of focussing on enjoyment of the beauty and wonder of the moment. It is also good to remember that in love there is no time nor distance and it is possible to broadcast love to those dear ones who are no longer dwelling on this plane of existence.

Bring in the Green Ray to help overcome any limiting attachments. Many anxieties are created in the heart through attachments. To attain peace of mind it is helpful to learn to enjoy whatever one has, but not to become so attached to it that you are shattered if it is taken away. Man comes penniless into this world and penniless he departs.

Meditation on the Green Ray will help develop discriminative qualities to overcome all indecisions. Any sense of discouragement will be transformed by the quality of hope inherent in the Green Ray. Hypocrisy, infirmities, egotism, covetousness, lustfulness and selfishness can all be overcome by the power of Green.

If an aura is dirty green, then insecurity will likely be the manifesting quality. Insecurity can lead to selfishness, attachment and possessive jealousy. A person may try to save and store money or his energy and become so much of a Scrooge that he gives nothing. Self-doubting tendencies are common for people with a negative green shade in their aura. Deceit, treachery, a double nature, mistrust of life—all are negative qualities of a dirty green aura that have to be dealt with and uprooted from consciousness.

Through meditation on the purity of green, we can call on our true expansive, compassionate, open-hearted natures. Open your heart to the Green Ray of brotherhood and prosperity. Helpful, gracious sympathy will begin to manifest in the heart, helping us to uplift others, that they may also love and respect themselves instead of being pulled into the mire. When the heart is open and we feel the love of the universe percolating through our being, we feel the greatest security and self confidence. We learn to love without any attachment or feelings of possessiveness. When we truly realize who and what we are, fears and doubts vanish. We can manifest the Divine Power because we realize we are eternally safe in the arms of the Infinite Father.

THE BLUE RAY
(Cervical or Throat Center)

If a person discovers that he is reactive to a situation and strikes out from an aggressive impulse, meditation on the Blue Ray will bestow the antidotes of quietude and restfulness. The pure Blue Ray holds the qualities of gentleness, contentment, patience, and composure.[4] If someone acts impulsively without stopping to think, jumping from experiencing one sensation to another, he needs to meditate on blue. All violent and restless people should bring the color of blue into their consciousnesses and feel its qualities of patience and composure.

If the aura is muddy blue and not clear, it is likely that the person is rigid and conservative. There will probably be slowness to respond and great resistance to change. It is often difficult for him to communicate feelings to others, as it takes such a person time to figure out what he is feeling. There may be fanatical adherence to dogma and very authoritarian communication to others. This authoritarian attitude may lead to a self-satisfied self-righteous type of personality. A blue-level person is orientated to the past and is often found searching through the vaults of history to find an ideal concept to rule his life by, instead of seeking guidance within. He often dwells in past memories instead of living spontaneously in the now. Pale blue in the aura indicates a very restful constitution, whereas deeper, intense blue indicates and induces reposeful activity. Bluish-grey indicates a fearful and timid nature. Religious impulses may be strong, but overshadowed by fear and misgiving.

Meditation on the Blue Ray of the Cosmic Light will transform us into peaceful, patient, contented, loyal, devotional persons. When clear blue sparkles in auras, it bestows deep spiritual understanding. The Blue Ray gives the power of synthesizing—bringing a combination of separate elements into a complex whole. This ability of a person with a blue aura allows him to seek through the scriptures and come up with the kernel of truth. Once the truth is found, he will tend to commit himself with great devotion and zeal to manifesting that ideal. The true blue of sincerity will manifest in all relationships of life. When we are sincere with ourselves, we can be sincere with others and with God.

THE INDIGO AND VIOLET RAY
(Medulla and Spiritual Eye and the
Thousand Petaled Lotus Center)

The Indigo and Violet Rays are a positive aid to people who are locked into the delusion of Maya.[5] Meditation on the spiritual colors of Indigo and Violet will help to uplift consciousnesses from preoccupation with the world of sensations. It will awaken realization of other planes of existence and other valid realities. Persons will begin to explore subtler energies within and around and release the self from chains of materialism. The doors to other states of consciousness will be opened, inviting exploration into their vastnesses.

If the Indigo Ray is not flowing smoothly and shows up as a muddy color in the aura, a person will be likely to show forgetful, inefficient, spaced-out tendencies. If someone is pre-occupied with the future, he tends to become introverted and very undisciplined, being unable to manifest things in the now. If the Violet Ray in the aura is distorted and appears cloudy, one can be lost in one's imagination and in castles in the sky. The man who shows a distorted Violet Ray will likely have a very negative self image.

When Indigo is bright and clear in the aura, we will find great intuitional, visionary abilities. Such a person is able to plan and make a reality of the vision of the future. Meditation on the Violet Ray and manifesting its light leads us toward a high spiritual attainment and holy love. Cosmic Consciousness and unconditional love for humanity are within grasp. We may then joyously find that creative imaginative power will mani-fest in all aspects of our lives.

Notes—Chapter 4

1. "Never in this world can hatred be stilled by hatred; it will be stilled only by non-hatred—this is the Law Eternal." Gautama Buddha

2. "When man has pity on all living creatures then only is he noble." Gautama Buddha

3. "No weapon can pierce the soul; no fire can burn it; no water can moisten it; nor can any wind wither it ... The soul is immutable, all-permeating, calm and immovable." Bhagavad-Gita 11:23–24

4. "He who is tranquil before friend and foe alike, and in adoration and insult, and during the experiences of warmth and chill and of pleasure and suffering ... that person is very dear to me." Bhagavad-Gita XII:18–19

5. Maya: The Hindu scripture term for cosmic delusion, Satan, or the law of relativity inherent in creation. The law of relativity or law of oppo-sites is present everywhere; heat and cold, light and shadow, pleasure and pain and so on.

5

Spiritual Unfoldment of the Divine Rays

THE ONE JOURNEY OF ALL RELIGIONS

THE DEEPER SPIRITUAL EXPERIENCES of the awakened chakra centers and Cosmic Rays can be better understood by studying and experiencing the eight-fold path of Patanjali,[1] the Revelations of Saint John and the *Interior Castle* of Saint Teresa of Avila. The basic steps of the yoga system of the Hindu philosophy are explained by Patanjali. They are: (1) moral proscriptions (yama), (2) right observances (niyama), (3) meditation posture (asana), (4) life force control (pranayama), (5) interiorization of the mind (pratyahara), (6) concentration (dharana), (7) meditation (dhyana), (8) union with God (samadhi). These are the necessary rungs on the ladder the devotee must climb to know God. Saint John's inner experiences in meditation were an unfolding of the seven spiritual centers represented by the seven churches. The seven candlesticks, churches and seals are symbols for the same thing. They are all symbolic of the seven cerebrospinal centers and the intelligence or Cosmic Ray residing in each center in the astral body of man.

These spinal centers are the seven trap-doors which, when opened, lead us back to God. Saint Teresa, who was one of the greatest of Christian mystics, describes each one of these states in her book, *The Interior Castle*. The first mansion which

Saint Teresa describes can be compared to the yama state of Patanjali and the first church of Ephesus of Saint John. These three descriptions are the experiences of the chakras and the manifestation of the intelligent consciousness of the Color Rays within. The parallel experiences of east and west are summarized in chart form on page 48.

It is to be pointed out that each individual is unique—a special, divine creation of God. No two grains of sand are exactly alike; each has its own distinct pattern. And so it is with the souls of men—we are all individuals and possess our own unique qualities and tendencies. God has created us all with some special attribute to discover, manifest, and perfect. In our evolution back to God, we all have a unique and special relationship with Spirit.

The experience we have within may be completely different from anyone else's, but it is just as valid. Certain experiences on the road to enlightenment are universal, but there is often great variation in the universal theme. In order to go back to God, we all have to travel the same highway of the spine, reversing the energy from the senses inward to the spinal centers and brain, where the presence of God may be felt. As we raise the energy of consciousness and awaken the seven cerebrospinal centers, we will at last find God in the innermost centers of our souls. The route is the same, but the experiences of each seeker may be vastly different, for we are all unique and equally loved by God. While Saint John had a vision of a white horse during the awakening of the coccygeal center, a Hindu might behold the form of Indra. Indra is yellow in color, four-armed, holding the wajra and a blue lotus in his hands and mounted on the white elephant, Airowata. Another may have a vision of a four-angled yellow figure and be attracted to the yellow color by opening this same center.

In essence the different experiences indicate cultural differences and variations in levels of concentration in meditation, which result in different revelations bestowed by God. Spirit

Revelations of East and West

Patanjali's eight fold path to God	Churches, Seals, Candlesticks, Angels and Spirits of Saint John	St. Theresa's spiritual experiences	Chakra Center Awakened	Cosmic Ray Manifested
Yama	Ephesus	The first mansion	Coccygeal	Red Ray
Niyama	Smyrna	The second mansion	Sacral	Orange Ray
Asana	Pergames	The third mansion	Lumbar or Solar Plexus	Yellow Ray
Pranayama	Thyatira	The fourth mansion	Dorsal or Heart	Green Ray
Pratyahara	Sardis	The fifth mansion	Cervical or Throat	Blue Ray
Dharana and Dhyana	Philadelphia	The sixth mansion	Medulla and Spiritual Eye	Indigo Ray
Samadhi	Laodicea	The seventh mansion	Thousand-Petaled Lotus in the Brain	Violet Ray and White Light

is inexhaustible; what is given to one devotee may not be given to another. Spirit has boundless treasures and God knows what we need and what we are ready to accept at each point in our evolution. We should not be concerned with the experiences we did or did not have in meditation. Our goal is to know and become one with God and manifest the qualities of the Divine Color Rays in our life.

THE FIRST CHURCH OR MANSION
The Coccygeal Center
(Red Ray)

Saint Teresa of Avila's description of the unfolding of the soul is beautifully described as the entering of an inner castle. "I began to think of the soul as if it were a castle made of a single diamond or of very clear crystal, in which there are many rooms, just as in Heaven there are many mansions . . . Let us now imagine that this castle, as I have said, contains many mansions, some above, others below, others at each side; and in the center and midst of them all is the chiefest mansion where the most secret things pass between God and the soul . . . You will have read certain books on prayer which advise the soul to enter within itself . . . As far as I can understand, the door of entry into this castle is prayer and meditation . . ." As one meditates and enters each one of these mansions, or churches, or chakra centers—and experiences the intelligent Cosmic Color Rays within—spiritual qualities begin to manifest. These qualities are represented by the eight-fold path of Patanjali.

When one's consciousness is centered in the first mansion or the coccygeal center, the ability to follow prohibitive rules is bestowed upon the individual. If this center and the Red Ray manifesting through it is misused, then negative, undesirable tendencies will result. In order to overcome the negative counterpart of this center, one must learn to go within and open up the divine qualities of the coccygeal, instead of letting the energy flow outward to identify with the restless, sensory world. The way to go within the inner sanctuary of the soul and to experience the positive qualities of the first mansion is through prayer and meditation.[2]

If we meditate and raise our energies and our consciousnesses to the first mansion, the power to abstain from negative thoughts and harmful actions will develop in us. We will manifest the spiritual qualities of the Red Ray. They are the five proscriptive moralities (Yama) as stated by Patanjali: avoidance of injury to others, of untruthfulness, of stealing, of incontinence, of gift-receiving (which brings obligations).

Saint Teresa of Avila states that the first mansion is also the center of self-knowledge and introspection, the ability to look at one's thoughts and actions and avoid the things that will later cause misery. Unfortunately most people do not learn from their mistakes and repeatedly experience the same problems over and over again, never correcting the causes in themselves. By the power of the Red Ray of self-knowledge a person may remove the obstacles in their road to happiness and may then advance quickly to a state of divine perfection.

When awakened, the first center causes the seed of true humility to grow in the consciousness. Humility needs to be nourished as each center is opened until one is purified in this sacred quality. Humility is not a feeling of worthlessness or guilt. It is simply seeing the divine magnitude of God and knowing how much one owes to Him.

At the end of this chapter are several charts which summarize some of the inner visions, sounds and other manifestations that are a result of opening up the various cerebrospinal centers. Check these charts for the coccygeal and the other centers as well to see if you have experienced anything similar.

THE SECOND CHURCH OR MANSION
The Sacral Center
(Orange Ray)

The opening of the sacral center and the manifestation of the Orange Ray gives the meditator the power to follow good rules and to overcome bad habits. Once experienced we will find that we are naturally drawn to practice the five positive prescriptions (Niyama) of Patanjali: purity of body and mind, contentment, self-discipline, self-study (contemplation), and devotion to God and Guru.

In the second mansion Saint Teresa of Avila describes how the consciousness is anxious to penetrate farther and become firmly established in the interior castle. It seeks every opportunity of advancement—by hearing uplifting sermons, engaging in edifying conversations, and associating with good company. The consciousness is adamant and does its utmost to practice virtue in its daily life.

Material attachments are very strong, and it is at this point of advancement on the spiritual path that negative tendencies or bad habits tend to rebel against the practice and cultivation of good ones. Bad habits are lodged as grooves in the subconscious mind. They must be rooted out, or they will continue their influence and cause us to act against our better judgments. The consciousness needs to be re-programmed by avoiding undesirable habits and practicing good rules, the positive qualities of the Red and Orange Ray. It is necessary to deliberately use and spiritualize the senses to bring about good. The eyes can best be used to see the good in all, ears to hear only truth, and taste trained to enjoy wholesome, energy-giving food.

When we experience the mental aspect of the Orange Ray, we realize the attributes of courage and confidence. It is helpful to manifest this quality in one's spiritual search for God when in meditation and all other activities. With great courage one needs to persevere and manifest and maintain good habits and overcome bad ones. With the strength of the Red Ray it is possible to avoid the things that have prevented us from obtaining ultimate satisfaction and joy. When we uplift our consciousnesses to the sacral center the power of the Orange Ray will spontaneously and automatically help us to follow good rules and overcome bad habits.

THE THIRD CHURCH OR MANSION
The Lumbar Center
(Yellow Ray)

When the purifying power of meditation has uplifted our consciousnesses and we are in tune with the lumbar or solar plexus centers, the quality of patience and self-control will awaken within us. If this center is misused, greed and unusual flesh temptations will surface. If we have attuned ourselves to the positive qualities of the Yellow Ray, we will begin to manifest a high standard of virtue. In the third mansion Saint Teresa tells us that the power of discipline will manifest and cause a spontaneous tendency towards acts of charity for others; while prudence, discretion and order will appear in our daily lives. This inner sense of control will manifest in all of our being—in the control of speech, dress and relationships with others.[3] We will experience an ever-increasing satisfaction in meditation and will want to set aside more and more time for this discipline. We will be extremely desirous of pleasing God in thought, word and deed.

Patanjali states that the purpose of an asana (meditation posture) is to rise above or stop the motions of the body. When motion ceases, Spirit begins to manifest Itself. Patanjali maintains that an erect spine is important as it allows the life energy and consciousness to flow freely from the lower centers of the senses, through the spine, to the higher mansions, or churches, or chakra centers and to the intelligent Cosmic Color Rays of spiritual realization. With the practice of asanas comes control over body and mind. We find that we practice self-control in all aspects of life when we allow the power of the Yellow Ray to manifest through our consciousnesses.

Saint Teresa states that the devotee who has reached the third mansion is motivated primarily by the inspiration of vision and reason, but has not as yet experienced the full inspiring force of love. He has not as yet totally surrendered himself and so his love is guided by the intellect and progress may be slow. If this is the point we have achieved, we may find we suffer from periods of aridity where we do not feel any devotion towards God or any inner joy. When we experience this state we need to summon all our self-control and go deeper into the spiritual life. Our greatest service to God is a resoluteness of will so that we continue to strive to know Him.

THE FOURTH CHURCH OR MANSION
The Dorsal Center
(Green Ray)

When our consciousnesses have risen to where they are manifesting in the heart or dorsal center, we begin to experience supernatural experiences or God's grace. In this state the soul-controlled life force and breath will appear. The dorsal is also the vitality and divine love center. Whenever anyone thinks of and is saturated with divine love and feels spiritual vitality he has activated the Green Ray of the dorsal center.

Up until this point our advancement in meditation has been due to our own efforts. Saint Teresa tells us in the fourth mansion God's grace takes a more active part. Once one has felt the presence of Spirit there is no doubt of our love for Him, for He is love itself. The conquering power of love now manifests in our lives. Love is the force that brings about profound changes in us and in the world. Love becomes more and more the essence of our consciousnesses as we progress spiritually. We find that we live it in all we do and proclaim it in all our words. It becomes a beacon light from the center of the heart which radiates to all and uplifts mankind Godward. The Green Ray is also the magnet that draws all divine blessings to us.[4]

Patanjali advocates Pranayama, which means conscious control of the life force, to be able ultimately to switch off at will the life force from the five senses. Christ said, "If thy hand or thy foot offend thee, cut it off and cast it from thee."[5] What He is saying is very scientific. If the sense of touch is bothering one's meditation then he or she should reverse the energy inward and disconnect himself from the distractions of it. The effectiveness of the practice of the technique of Pranayama will be shown in how much energy is withdrawn from the senses upward into the spine and how quiet the mind becomes.

Saint Teresa of Avila and the Carmelite nuns did not practice scientific yoga techniques; they practiced mental prayer. It was through God's grace that they experienced the power of the Green Ray: the withdrawal of the life force within. She describes in the fourth mansion of her interior castle the results of the soul-controlled life force. She tells us that this state of awakening is God's grace and is bestowed upon us when He wills. These experiences often come when we least expect it. Suddenly we find understanding is suspended and will is absorbed and in some mysterious or unknown way united with the Will of God. We feel as if we have been drawn within and are absorbed in the peace and sweetness of soul. This suspension or upward pull is at first confusing and may even be frightening, but it is so delectable an absorption that we quickly realize that we would not wish to be in any other situation for any amount of money in the world.

Whether through conscious control of Pranayama or God's grace one's consciousness is uplifted to the heart center, the devotee will experience the interiorization of the life force. Spirit will no longer be an intellectual concept or mental image but felt as a living reality in the temple of one's consciousness.

THE FIFTH CHURCH OR MANSION
The Cervical Center
(Blue Ray)

The seven churches and candlesticks that Saint John mentions in Revelations are the chakra centers in the body and the seven stars are the Cosmic Color Rays radiating through these centers. By the power of meditation we can activate the Blue Star Ray by opening the throat center and the qualities of calmness and devotion will manifest in our consciousnesses. The kingdom of peace is established in the soul as the once restless, sense-distracted mind is absorbed within into a state of tranquility.[6] When we feel cosmic energy and cosmic vibration our consciousnesses are focussed in the cervical center. We will want to work to keep the Blue Cosmic Ray from distortion and to learn to express its positive essence at all times.

Saint Teresa calls the opening of this center the Prayer of Union or the Spiritual Bethrothal. Patanjali refers to this state as Pratyahara: the power of mental interiorization or withdrawal of the mind from the senses. Pranayama—life force control—leads to Pratyahara—interiorization of consciousness. In this state the mind is disconnected from physical sensations and is under the control of the meditator. When one has reached this state then he can control body, moods and habits at will.

In the fourth mansion Saint Teresa explains that the soul is completely lost to the world for short durations and is possessed by God. The consciousness is withdrawn so far from the body it is hard to tell if there is still breath and life in it. The body becomes immobile and the imagination, memory and understanding are no longer obstacles to the blessings received from

God. We find ourselves free from all distractions—nothing can penetrate the castle of the soul. The feeling of bliss is then felt within, right to the marrow of our bones. We experience an unquestionable certainty that we have known God and it is not a figment of the imagination. All the sense faculties are lost; we realize from the depths of the soul that it is our will that has been absorbed in the Will of God. We cannot rationalize how the experience happens; all we know is that our will has somehow been united with God's Will. We still feel separate from Him, but know that there has been a union of wills.

The results of the union with Spirit in this state are innumerable. We become aware that the soul is like an eagle in flight and it is now possessed with a continual yearning and longing to be with the beloved of its heart, God. Saint Teresa relates that we may sometimes feel despair, for it seems we are stuck between two worlds. We often find it difficult to associate with things of the world and feel weary of this plane of existence as we yearn to be with God all the time. The soul is no longer bound by ties of relationships, friendship or property. At the same time, we feel set on doing God's Will and giving everything to Him. Once we become absorbed in the Prayer of Union our whole motive will be to serve God by serving others. Whenever opportunity presents itself, we will help our neighbor in need.

THE SIXTH CHURCH OR MANSION
The Medulla and Spiritual Eye Center
(Indigo Ray)

The spiritual eye is the door to God, the center of will in man and the seat of intuition. When consciousness is attuned to this center we become absorbed in the Indigo Ray and aware of some cosmic manifestation of God such as love, wisdom, joy, light or the Om vibration. In the Yoga Sutras of

Patanjali he states that Dharana is the power to use the interiorized mind one-pointedly to concentrate on God.

If we have been meditating on the Holy Ghost we may begin to hear the Cosmic Sound within the ears of the soul. As the vibration becomes louder it will encompass our heads and then our whole bodies will vibrate in tune with the Holy Ghost or Om. We begin to feel our consciousness becoming one with the Om vibration in every atom of creation, first in our immediate surroundings, then everywhere. Put some dye in water and what happens? The dye spreads throughout the water. When we open the spiritual eye our consciousness begins to spread everywhere. If our expansion of consciousness takes place with the quality of love, we feel and we become one with the love present in every heart. We will then identify with love itself and become one with the universe of love, experiencing all the love of the cosmos simultaneously.

In the sixth mansion Saint Teresa conveys how raptures consume the soul and the breath may be sucked out of the body. From time immemorial yogis have said that in the breathless state Spirit manifests Itself. "The position, in this case, as I understand it, is that the soul has never before been so fully awake to the things of God or had such light or such knowledge of His Majesty. This may seem impossible; because, if the faculties are so completely absorbed that we might describe them as dead, and the senses are so as well, how can the soul be said to understand this secret?" The secret is known by the all-knowing faculty of the soul—intuition—the manifestation of the Indigo Ray. "For when He (God) means to enrapture this soul, it loses its power of breathing, with the result that, although its other senses sometimes remain active a little longer, it cannot possibly speak. At other times it loses all its powers at once, and the hands and the body grow so cold that the body seems no longer to have a soul—sometimes it even seems doubtful if there is any breath in the body. This lasts only for a short time (I mean, only for a short period at any one time) because, when this profound suspension lifts a little, the body seems to come partly to itself again, and draws breath, though only to die once more, and, in doing so, to give fuller life to the soul. Complete ecstasy, therefore, does not last long . . . the ecstasy has the effect of leaving the will so completely absorbed and the understanding so completely transported—for as long as a day, or even for several days—that the soul seems incapable of grasping anything that does not awaken the will to love . . ."

It is by the Indigo Ray of Intuition that we can behold God and understand the mysteries of the universe. Saint Teresa tells us in the sixth mansion that consciousness has access to the divine library of universal knowledge. "In a single instant he is taught so many things all at once that, if he were to labor for years on end in trying to fit them all into his imagination and thought, he could not succeed with a thousandth part of them."

THE SEVENTH CHURCH OR MANSION
The Thousand-Petaled Lotus Center
(Violet Ray and White Light)

When the thousand-petaled lotus or crown center is open, then the Violet Ray and White Light of spiritual perfection will manifest. We become one with God and will have fulfilled the purpose of our existence. Cosmic Consciousness is our true nature and by reclaiming our divine heritage we become one with the ocean of God and the waves of creation as well. We are aware of and work through our bodies, yet still are immersed in the vastness of God. We are the universe and the infinite vibrationless Spirit beyond. We realize the meaning of "My Father and I are One." We become one with the eternal now; everything past, present and future is in our consciousnesses. We are aware of a tree, the sun, our bodies and the Infinite Spirit simultaneously and know that we are the tree, sun, body and Infinite Spirit. No longer do we feel separation from God, or from his creation. Every thought that has ever been or will be thought is known to us. There is nothing that we are not aware of. We are everything and everything is in us. Our tiny spark of consciousness has become the fire of infinity. Our minds reflect the Eternal Mind of God. We are perfect peace. Every scale has been removed from the eyes of the soul. Our soul has been united with Spirit and cannot be separated anymore.

Patanjali declares that Dhyana gives the conception, by intuition or feeling, of the vastness of God. The supreme state of consciousness is samadhi or complete union with God. Saint Teresa calls this sublime state spiritual marriage. The spiritual betrothal of the fifth and sixth mansions is transformed into complete union in the seventh mansion. Saint Teresa uses a descriptive metaphor to describe the spiritual betrothal and the ultimate perfection of spiritual marriage. "The spiritual betrothal is different: here the two persons are frequently separated, as is the case with union, for, although by union is meant the joining of two things into one, each of the two, as is a matter of common observation, can be separated and remain a thing by itself. This favor of the Lord passes quickly and afterwards the soul is deprived of that companionship— I mean so far as it can understand. In this other favor of the Lord it is not so: the soul remains all the time in that center with its God. We might say that union is as if the ends of two wax candles were joined so that the light they give is one: the wicks and the wax and the light are all one; yet afterwards the one candle can be perfectly well separated from the other and the candles become two again, or the wick may be withdrawn from the wax. But here it is like rain falling from the heavens into a river or a spring; there is nothing but water there and it is impossible to divide or separate the water belonging to the river from that which fell from the heavens. Or it is as if a tiny streamlet enters the sea, from which it will find no way of separating itself, or as if in a room there were two large windows through which the light streamed in: it enters in different places but it all becomes one."

INNER EXPERIENCES OF THE
SEVEN MANSIONS
(Seven Color Rays)

By proper diet and other health measures we can stimulate the efficient functioning of the pranas or life forces in the body. These are metabolizing, crystalizing, assimilating, circulating, eliminating. By proper diet and meditation we can convert the differential life currents into ONE LIFE FORCE by drawing them into the spine and brain, and uniting them with COSMIC LIFE. Through meditation and control of the energy in our bodies we can convert the vibrations of the solid physical body into astral energy. In other words, when we bring all the currents from the senses into the coiled passage in the spine it will flow in the Ida and Pingala and then into the Susumna in the spine. From there the one current will flow out the medulla to the infinite, carrying the soul with it. All the energy in one's consciousness is gathered and changed into Cosmic Consciousness.

As the energy retires within and up the spine, the seven centers will open and the dropping lotus-petaled rays will be raised upward. One may know which chakra one's consciousness is in by the divine qualities manifesting, as we have already seen. Various colors, sounds and visions may be perceived. The different currents working in the centers manifest different sounds and by hearing these sounds one may come in contact with the chakra centers. The Red Ray—earth current or eliminating current—of the coccygeal emanates a sound like a buzzing bee. All vibrations produce a sound according to their rate of frequency and are also endowed with a color.

Saint John talked of these divine sounds when he said, "I was in the Spirit on the Lord's day and heard behind me a great voice, as of a trumpet."[7] This trumpet is the sound of the Holy Ghost or Om heard when one's consciousness is attuned to the medulla oblongata and its polar opposite, the spiritual eye. Saint John also talks about harpers harping with their harps which is the sound from a different center. By concentrating on these manifestations and trying to become one with them we will uplift our consciousnesses and be drawn closer to God. Each revelation within needs to be respected and our single-pointed concentration must be put into this process so we will reap the highest harvest in our meditation. Concentrating on just one manifestation—a sound or color or feeling—could lead to our salvation. As different spokes of a wheel meet in the hub at the center, so these different manifestations lead to the supreme goal of life: God Himself. Let us look at the Color Rays manifesting through the spinal centers and their various qualities.

THE SEVEN MANSIONS
(Seven Color Rays)

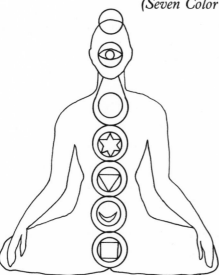

The Higher Centers

When we are in touch with these centers we are operating through intuition, intelligence and discrimination.

We begin to manifest the inner divine qualities of the soul: love, peace, joy, power, humility, compassion, devotion, intuition, discrimination, omniscience and omnipresence.

The Three Lower Centers

All material sensations work through the three lower centers.

The negative aspects of the three centers work through a mind identified with the senses and produce restlessness, material desires, sense attachments and negative tendencies.

If we are mentally negative or neutral or preoccupied or identified with sex thoughts, we are working through the three material centers in connection with the skin's surface.

The eight meannesses of the heart are from association with the negative aspect of the lower centers: fear, shame, grief, hatred, condemnation, family pride, race prejudice, a narrow sense of responsibility.

When one's consciousness is identified with the three lower centers it is important to concentrate on and manifest the qualities of strength, courage, intelligence and joy.

THE ELEMENTS AND INNER SOUNDS[8]
MANIFESTING IN THE SEVEN MANSIONS

Thousand-Petaled Lotus (Violet and White Light)	The seat of ultimate realization. The awareness of infinite bliss and space. The soundless sound.
Medulla Oblongata and Spiritual Eye (Indigo Ray)	The super ether element or energy (through which thoughts and life force travel) is manifested. The inner sound is the Om vibration which is the combination of all sounds. The basic vibration from which all creation is structured.
Cervical or Throat (Blue Ray)	The etheric element is manifested in the cervical center.

The sound of an ocean roar is heard in meditation.

Dorsal or Heart
(Green Ray)

The air or vitality element is manifested in the dorsal center.
The inner sound of the astral bell is heard in meditation.

Lumbar or Solar Plexus
(Yellow Ray)

The fire element is manifested in the lumbar center.
The inner sound of the astral harp is heard in meditation.

Sacral
(Orange Ray)

The water element is manifested in the sacral center.
The inner sound of the astral flute is heard in meditation.

Coccygeal
(Red Ray)

The earth element is manifested in the coccygeal center.
The inner sound like the drone of a bumblebee is heard in meditation.

INNER REALIZATIONS OF THE
SEVEN MANSIONS
(Seven Color Rays)

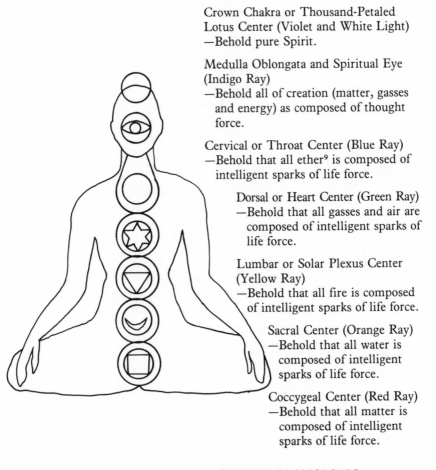

Crown Chakra or Thousand-Petaled Lotus Center (Violet and White Light) —Behold pure Spirit.

Medulla Oblongata and Spiritual Eye (Indigo Ray) —Behold all of creation (matter, gasses and energy) as composed of thought force.

Cervical or Throat Center (Blue Ray) —Behold that all ether[9] is composed of intelligent sparks of life force.

Dorsal or Heart Center (Green Ray) —Behold that all gasses and air are composed of intelligent sparks of life force.

Lumbar or Solar Plexus Center (Yellow Ray) —Behold that all fire is composed of intelligent sparks of life force.

Sacral Center (Orange Ray) —Behold that all water is composed of intelligent sparks of life force.

Coccygeal Center (Red Ray) —Behold that all matter is composed of intelligent sparks of life force.

VISIONS OF THE SEVEN MANSIONS
(Seven Color Rays)

This chart (see p. 66) is not to be followed strictly, but is offered as an aid to knowing that such experiences exist. If some of these visions appear, then know that your concentration has deepened and you are in touch with one of the spinal centers and its inherent Color Ray. As Spirit is infinite, so there are infinite possible ways It may manifest Its presence. Devotees may have different visions than these as they attain different levels of concentration.

It is good to remember it is not the number of visions a person has that determines his spirituality, but what he does with his life. Is one kind instead of being arrogant? Does one manifest evenmindedness and calmness in all phases of life? These are the questions persons should ask to see if they are growing spiritually.

OTHER MANIFESTATIONS OF THE DIVINE RAYS ACCORDING TO PATANJALI

Patanjali mentions various powers in his yoga sutras.

- The power to reduce anything as small as we like including our own body and the power to magnify anything as large as we like. We can magnify it to an infinite dimension or shrink it to an infinitesimal size.

- The power to make anything as light in weight as we wish including our own body and the power to make anything as heavy as we wish.

- The power of obtaining any object of our desire.

- The power to bring everything under our control.

- The power of satisfying all our desires by the use of our own will power.

- The power of becoming one with God—Lord over everything.

Visions of the Seven Mansions
(Seven Color Rays)

	Visions of Saint John	*Visions of the Yogis*	
		Color	*Form*
Thousand-Petaled Lotus (Violet and White Light)	Angel opening the thousand-petaled lotus center.	Vision of Cosmic Consciousness.	Vision of One's Guru. Deity Paramashiya.
Medulla Oblongata and Spiritual Eye (Indigo Ray)	Earthquake and an angel opening this center.	Spiritual Eye—a white pulsating star in the center of a blue ring. Golden ring surrounding the blue ring.	Deity Hakini (white color) six-armed, seated on a white lotus. Deity Shambhu.
Cervical or Throat (Blue Ray)	Beholding the souls of the perfected slain. Angel opening this center.	Smoke color with luminous sparks of light.	Deity Ambara (white color) four-armed, seated on a white elephant. Deity Sadashiva.
Dorsal or Heart (Green Ray)	Pale Horse. Angel opening this center.	A palpitating blue ball.	Deity Wayu (smoke colored) four-armed, seated on a black antelope. Deity Ishwara.

Lumbar or Solar Plexus (Yellow Ray)	Black Horse. Angel opening this center.	Blood red triangle.	Deity Wahni (shining red) four-armed, seated on a ram. Deity Vishnu.
Sacral (Orange Ray)	Red Horse. Angel opening this center.	White half-moon.	Deity Waruna (white color) four-armed, seated on a mokara. Deity Rudra.
Coccygeal (Red Ray)	White Horse. Angel opening this center.	Yellow figure with four angles.	Deity Indra (yellow color) four-armed, on a white elephant. Deity Brahma.

Notes—Chapter 5

1. Patanjali: Ancient exponent of yoga, whose eightfold yoga system is outlined in his Yoga Sutras.

2. "It is a reminder to ourselves that we are helpless without God's support. No effort is complete without prayer, without a definite recognition that the best human endeavor is of no effect if it has not God's blessing behind it. Prayer is a call to humility. It is a call to self-purification, to inward search." Gandhi

3. "The man who is calm and even-minded during pain and pleasure, the one whom these cannot ruffle, he alone is fit to attain everlastingness. Bhagavad-Gita 11:15

4. "The true measure of loving God is to love Him without measure." St. Bernard

5. Matthew 18:8

6. "With virtue and quietness one may conquer the world." Lao-Tzu

7. Revelations 1:10

8. The inner astral sounds from the spine are heard by intuition. They are beyond the range of the senses.

9. All elemental vibrations of matter in the body are a result of the Cosmic Rays flowing into and through the different spinal centers.

6

The Color Attributes
of the World Cycles

*EVOLUTIONARY CYCLES
AND THEIR COLORS*

Everything in creation is striving for perfection. The soul made in the Image of God is perfect and will ultimately settle for nothing less than perfection. How do we know that Spirit exists and dwells within us? Our drive for perfection in a seemingly unperfect world indicates to us the presence of a Transcendent Intelligence within ourselves. The Supreme Intelligence of God operates in every level of creation. He is striving to bring everything to a state of perfect unfoldment or perfection. As we open up each chakra and manifest the perfect potential of each cosmic ray, so this planet must pass through various cycles to achieve the highest utopian perfection.

As the planets and their moons revolve around the sun, so the sun revolves around a fixed star and it in turn around the cosmic center of the universe. The cosmic center is the projection booth of the cosmos where Spirit projects divine color rays to structure and maintain the universe. Where the play of light first manifests is the central point of the universe. Our sun and planets revolve around this center and when our planetary system is closest to this point, then the evolution of mankind is most highly advanced. When we are furthest away from this center, mankind's evolution is at its lowest ebb.

As the signs of the zodiac are created by the earth revolving around the sun, so the macrocosmic zodiac is created by our sun revolving around the cosmic center. At present we are in the Pisces-Virgo age and are advancing into the Aquarius-Leo age. Pisces and Aquarius are in the Autumnal Equinox and their opposite signs Virgo and Leo respectively are in the Vernal Equinox. Every twelve years, as the sun moves closer to the grand center, there is a refinement in the brain structure of all of humanity. This evolution will continue until we have reached the closest proximity to the grand center. When we have reached this point all knowledge will be easily within our grasp—even the unfathomable secrets of Spirit. As the sun moves away from the grand center everything will experience a de-evolution. When the sun is at the furthest point away from the cosmic center mankind will be so basic that nothing will be understood beyond the world of sensations.

There are seven cycles which are related to the seven color manifestations of the chakras. The Bhuloka cycle is the red level of evolution. This level or stage of creation is also known as Kali Yuga. The evolution of this planet will continue to progress through these stages until it reaches the highest per-fected Golden Age. When the world is in a particular stage of development, then the consciousness of the majority of the people on that planet is the same. Our planet is advancing toward the cosmic center and has just recently entered the second stage of evolution of Bhuvarloka or Dwapara Yuga. The seven evolutionary levels are as follows:

Color	Age or Cycle	Vernal Equinox	Autumnal Equinox
Red Level	Bhuloka or Kali Yuga	Pisces	Virgo
Orange Level	Bhuvarloka or Dwapara Yuga	Pisces Aquarius	Virgo Leo
Yellow Level	Swarloka or Treta Yuga	Aquarius Capricorn Sagittarius	Leo Cancer Gemini
Green Level	Maharloka or Satya Yuga (Golden Age)	Sagittarius	Gemini
Blue Level	Janaloka or Satya Yuga (Golden Age)	Scorpio	Taurus
Indigo Level	Tapoloka or Satya Yuga (Golden Age)	Scorpio Libra	Taurus Aries
Violet Level	Satyaloka or Satya Yuga (Golden Age)	Libra	Aries

THE RED CYCLE
(Bhuloka—Kali Yuga)

This is known as the dark or materialistic age. The planet and mankind's hearts in general are very dark. Man is deeply engrossed in ignorance and is aware of the physical world of gross matter only. He is barbaric and crude, concentrating only on satisfying the senses. Around five hundred A.D. this planet was at its furthest point away from the cosmic center of the universe. The history of this era is filled with tales of the lack of morality and virtue with little peace manifesting anywhere.[1]

THE ORANGE CYCLE
(Bhuvarloka—Dwapara Yuga)

Mankind in general at this point of evolution understands the finer subtler forces of the energies or the properties of the electricities. These electrical powers are now being tapped and used by instruments for many practical purposes. When this age is fully manifested not only will man discover and use these electricities but will understand all their attributes and qualities. The treatment and healing of disease will be through vibratory rays in this age.

Mankind in general will be aware of his inner energies as His consciousness will not remain entirely engrossed in the outward material world. Peace will become more established but there is ever the danger of using electrical discoveries for destructive reasons in this cycle.

THE YELLOW CYCLE
(Swarloka—Treta Yuga)

The yellow cycle is the mental age and most people will use the power of the mind in all phases of life. With the advance of mind power the use of electricity will lessen. Mind power will be used as a medium for healing and sustenance for the body. Wisdom will be awakened and people will live more respectfully and peacefully with each other.

Mankind at this stage of evolution will be able to comprehend the qualities of divine magnetism which create the electrical forces. Mankind in this state is established in the inner worlds and understands the inner electricities, magnetic poles and auras. He understands the spiritualized heart and the darkness of maya or delusion.

THE GREEN CYCLE
(Maharloka—Satya Yuga)

Mankind in general is no longer a puppet of delusion and is able to behold the Light of Spirit which is the only reality.

THE BLUE CYCLE
(Janaloka—Satya Yuga)

Mankind at this stage of evolution is highly purified in consciousness and not only beholds the Light of Spirit but becomes one with it and manifests it in his life. He realizes he is a Son of God, and one with the Christ Consciousness in every atom of creation.

THE INDIGO CYCLE
(Tapoloka—Satya Yuga)

Mankind merges his consciousness in the Holy Ghost and becomes dead to the idea of any separate existence from the Holy Spirit. He is immersed in the consciousness of the Holy Ghost or Om.

THE VIOLET CYCLE
(Satyaloka—Satya Yuga)

Mankind beholds that he is one with God and that all of creation is nothing but his own Self. The statement mankind is made in the Image of God, is no longer a poetic nicety for him but a living reality.

Notes—Chapter 6

1. See *The Holy Science* by Swami Sri Yukteswar.

7

Color and the Arts

COLOR AND MUSIC

In the *Scientific American* it was reported that microsound is definitely associated with light and color frequencies. We have stated that all vibrations have a color, a sound and an intelligence. Each note on the musical scale has a corresponding color and every color has a corresponding note. Sound and color are the same thing perceived by different senses. It is a perception of vibration. Very often people who hear music see different colors. The frequency of the music heard has stimulated the perception of the color of that frequency.

The relationship of the notes and colors has been worked out mathematically by the laws of physics and has been found to correspond to what sensitives have seen when hearing different music. Middle C is red, D is orange, E is yellow, F is green, G is blue, A is indigo and B is violet. The note F# which is in between F and G is a combination of F green and G blue which would be turquoise. If we play a chord—for example the A chord—that chord will manifest three colors. The E note manifests yellow, A, indigo and C# a combination of red and orange. If we play the notes upward on the piano scale, the colors produced will become lighter and more ethereal as we move up. If we play the notes downward on the scale the colors become deeper and more gem like.

Vibration Relationship of the
Spectrum of Colors

Color	Key Note	Quality Intelligence	Center
Red	C	Strength, Power, Life and Vitality	Coccygeal
Orange	D	Optimism, Self-Confidence, Enthusiasm and Courage; the Social Ray	Sacral
Yellow	E	Mental Power and Joy	Lumbar or Solar Plexus
Green	F	Love, Balance, Harmony, Peace, Brotherhood, Hope, Growth and Healing	Dorsal or Heart
Blue	G	Inspiration, Creativity, Spiritual Understanding, Faith and Devotion	Cervical or Throat
Indigo	A	Spiritual Perception, Intuition	Spiritual Eye and Medulla Oblongata
Violet	B	Divine Realization, Humility, Creative Imagination	Crown or Thousand-Petaled Lotus
White	All Notes	All Qualities	Crown or Thousand-Petaled Lotus

The qualities of color that we have studied can be trans-
posed to the corresponding key notes, C is strength and vitality,
D is courage and enthusiasm and so on. If we remember the
physical healing properties of the colors, we can see that F is
good for calming the nerves, whereas G is good for calming
the mind and F# is beneficial in helping form new skin. F
vibrates to green, G vibrates to blue and F# vibrates to turquoise. By selecting music in a particular key we can use it
to stimulate various qualities and healing in our life. Often it is
not the key the music is written in, but the predominant note
in the music that will depict the mood and stimulate the healing. A person with a bright green aura will be attracted to the
note of F. These notes in turn affect the corresponding chakra
centers: F activates the heart, E the solar plexus, D the lumbar and so on.

Let us think about the power of sound and color vibration.
Caruso shattered a glass by singing a long, high, sustained
note. The walls of Jericho fell down when a ram's horn was
played by the priests. An article in the United Press entitled,
"Sing Away" relates the use of music by the Navajo medicine
men. They change the frequency of the ill person's body from
a disharmony into a harmony with the universe with sound.
Sometimes they may sing for five to seven days—a total of
fifty to one hundred hours—to help correct very serious ill-
nesses. Often the whole family joins in the singing. The successful mantras of Indian rain dance ceremonies show how the
help of nature can be enlisted by using sound vibrations
properly.

Through sensitive instruments science has discovered that
the sound of growing grass is F. By playing F—which vibrates
to nature's color green—we can help plants grow stronger.
It is possible through color and sound to stimulate and heal
every cell in the body, activate the elements of nature and,
when practiced with devotion and love, to attract the supreme
Lord of the Universe to us.

COLOR AND ART

From the ideas of Supreme Intelligence came the beauties and marvels of creation. Man is made in the Image of God and has within his being unlimited creative potential. Creativity is an inherent quality of the soul and man's natural urge as a soul is to express that creativity. In the final emancipation when one has established himself in God consciousness he will be able to create worlds even as Spirit does.

In the astral realm one is able to create at will. If one wishes to create a garden or a tree, one can materialize this from pure thought. The astral realm is composed of light or prana and can be molded by the will of its inhabitants. In this realm everything reflects the beauty and harmony of the Creator. Man's higher creativity not only desires to materialize itself but also to create the highest form of perfection and beauty. One may see this in great masterpieces of art. They have the power to uplift and transform man's consciousness from the mundane to the supernal realms. As one gazes at them their energy is unmistakably felt and is healing.

Mankind in general, however, identifies with and is attached to the body. The soul's creative expression becomes deluded and manifests in a desire for and preoccupation with sex. As one's consciousness turns back towards the Creator one's creativity functions on higher planes. Art is an expression of this higher creativity and self-fulfillment. However, so long as man is attached to the body with its corresponding thoughts, moods and emotions, his attitudes will be reflected in his creative expression in art. All great masters have created from the superconscious mind and have not limited themselves to the conscious and subconscious only. The superconscious mind is the treasure house of man where he is in touch with the divine qualities of the soul. When a person creates from this plane of consciousness then the qualities of peace, balance and harmony will manifest in the art form.

Man is evolving in consciousness and so is his expression in art. In ancient times man was aware of a limited color spectrum. As he evolves, his ability to perceive other vibratory frequencies has opened up a greater range of color vibrations. Through evolution the awareness of color will become subtle and ethereal. Working with color is in itself transforming. As we have mentioned so often, color has an intelligence. When one works from one's soul, then the intelligence of the soul will work in harmony with the intelligence of color to produce a creation that is uplifting to all of humanity. If one works from one's ego, however, what is likely to be expressed is one's suppressed frustrations and anxieties. The attraction will tend to be to dark, muddy shades of color with no uplifting or inspiring content. The result may be a lowering of the viewer's consciousness.

A painter can heal himself and others through his paintings. Disease is nothing more than a disharmony of frequency in one's being that brings on an imbalance in glandular function or in the functioning of the psyche. Through negative thoughts and emotions the harmonious balance of the body can be altered. A persistent negative attitude brings on chronic problems. Color is energy and by working with color and gazing at inspired paintings the proper frequency alignment may be stimulated in mind and body.

Disease can often be a result of color frequency starvation. By absorbing oneself with the needed color balance may be attained. Too much of one color can be counteracted by the complementary color. The Egyptian healing temples used rooms with certain shapes and colors that corresponded to certain body areas and afflictions. By being in these rooms the healing vibrations would bathe the patient's consciousness.

A painter who is in tune with his intuitive Self could produce a painting that could heal various afflictions. Above all the God-conscious artist could inspire others to attain their highest fulfillment—oneness with God. Leonardo Da Vinci

wrote in one of his notebooks that the highest and most difficult aim of painting is to depict "the intention of man's soul"
through gestures and movements of the limbs—a dictum not
to be interpreted as referring to momentary emotional states,
but to man's inner life as a whole. Leonardo's Last Supper is
one of the greatest manifestations of his philosophy.

Heinrich Hoffman's painting of Christ at Thirty-Three
is impregnated with a holy vibration. The quality of compassion in Christ's face could not have been portrayed unless
Hoffman felt the essence of Christ in his own life. Christ's
eyes are so transfiguring they could only have been painted
by a man of realization. A painting such as this has been
created out of the depths of true devotion to God and will
therefore spiritually uplift the beholder. The beholder, feeling
uplifted from the holy vibrations of the painting, will be inspired to seek the Supreme Artist.

8

The Physical Expression of the Divine Rays

THE PHYSICAL ESSENCE

IN ESSENCE THE BODY is not flesh, but energy. Bodily functions are sustained by Cosmic Energy entering the medulla oblongata and working through the different chakra centers. If this energy were removed, our physical bodies would cease to operate. Most people think of the body as so many pounds of flesh and do not perceive its true essence. If we understood that we are the product of seven cosmic currents we could rejuvenate and heal ourselves at will.

If a primitive man were taken to a movie he would think the actors on the screen are real and would be caught up in the drama before him. If you told him they were not real he would not believe you. The only way to convince him would be to take him to the screen and tell him to touch it. Another way to show him it is a delusion would be to take him up to the projection booth and show him that the scenes are a result of the light rays emanating out of the film projector. He might then clearly see that the actors were only a play of light on the projection screen.

Similarily God has projected the play of creation out of Himself and His ideas are mirrored in light on the screen of space. The only way to convince ourselves that this world that seems so real to our five senses is a delusive state is to take our attention from the screen of creation to the projection booth of the spine. The colossal projection booth is the heart of the infinite, but there are sub-reflectors in the body of man. Each spinal center projects a current that carries out a particular function in the body. If we reverse our energy and thus our consciousness and attention to the spine, we will see the body as a play of light carrying on all the functions necessary to maintain life.

Let us look at the function of our inner processes of life. The duty of the senses is to identify with and operate in the physical creation before us. It is the mind that co-ordinates the information received by the senses. The life force within keeps the body, mind and senses working together in a co-ordinated, harmonious unit. The function of intelligence and conscience is to determine what is useful and best to maintain our lives. Cosmic Energy sustains the five astral and the five physical senses, seven life currents or Cosmic Rays, mind and intelligence. Intuition's highest call is to tune in with the Will of God and manifest it in our lives.

The individual spherical dynamos of energy in the spine are known as the chakras. Their function is to structure and maintain the twenty-seven thousand-billions of individual cells in our bodies. If the life force is not properly distributed from the thousand rays of the crown chakra in the brain to the individual chakras in the spine because of blockages, the life currents cannot structure the different vibrating elements which make up the human body. The frequency at the biological level slows down and when the cells are not properly charged they divide and may create tumors.

Each chakra center has a certain number of petals which indicate the number of rays of life current emanating from that center to perform various functions in the body. The coccygeal has four rays, the sacral has six, the lumbar has ten, the dorsal has twelve, the cervical has sixteen, the medulla has two and the crown chakra has a thousand rays. Some of the functions of the various centers and life forces are as follows:

THE RAYS

Red Ray
Coccygeal—Earth Current   The current flowing through the coccygeal is the force responsible for solidifying the life force into atoms of flesh.

Eliminating Current—   When this current is not functioning properly it creates intestinal and stomach gases, constipation, tumors, boils, pimples, carbuncles and poor appetite.

Orange Ray
Sacral—Water Current   This current structures and sustains the atoms of the watery circulatory substances in the body.

Circulating Current   When this current is malfunctioning pernicious anemia and skin troubles result.

Yellow Ray
Lumbar—Fire Current   This current maintains the electronic and astral heat in the body.

Assimilating Current—   When this current is not flowing properly it causes indigestion and constipation.

Green Ray
Dorsal—Air Current   The air current enables the oxygen and air elements to combine with the body cells.

Crystalizing Current—   When this current is not flowing properly the result is tuberculosis etc.

Blue Ray
Cervical—Ether Current   This current maintains the etheric
                               background in the body for trans-
                               mission of sounds and electrons.
Metabolistic Current   When this current is not flowing
                               properly the bodily organs begin to
                               dry up, lungs collapse, intestines
                               shrink and adhesions result.

Indigo Ray
Medulla and Spiritual   The super ether is used for the trans-
Eye—Ether (Super)   mission of thoughts and life force.

Cosmic Energy—   Cosmic Energy enters the body at
                               this point and sustains all functions
                               of life. If this current fails to enter
                               the body then there can be no life.

Violet Ray and White
Light
Thousand-Petaled Lotus   Cosmic Energy is stored in this
                               center. It is the main switch that
                               allows the thousand rays of life cur-
                               rent to maintain the thousand func-
                               tions of the body.

Whenever there is a physical problem we need to meditate
and call on the Cosmic Current and Intelligence to rearrange
the atoms and electrons that are out of order in the cells. The
Divine Light flowing through the chakras affects the nerve
plexus and causes the endocrine glands to secrete hormones.
These hormones affect our different states of consciousness,
personality and bodily functions. By controlling the life force
currents flowing through our spinal centers we can bring about
whatever changes we wish. Taking in chemicals and medicines
can only affect the outer structure of the bodily cells, but

cannot alter the inner atomic structure or the life essence contained within the cells. Often no healing is possible until the pure beam of Spirit changes and rearranges the atoms to bring about a state of healing and peace.

We are aware of color as a result of sensations, perception, conception and thought. The awareness of color is strictly a mental process as color is part of our consciousness. When the reflected rays from an object stimulate the eye, the impulse is taken to the brain and we recognize color because the Cosmic Color Rays are already manifesting within us.

In early primitive civilizations man was able to perceive only a few colors, but through evolution he has acquired the ability to see a wider range of hues. The further we advance the greater will be our receptiveness to colors or vibrations. The hues and brilliance will become more dazzling and breathtaking. As man evolves, he begins to open up the chakra centers and allow the Cosmic Rays to flow through his being. It is said that the refinement of the brain structure is increased ever so slightly every twelve years for all mankind. Even with obedience to the laws of nature it will take us a million years to reach Cosmic Consciousness, the ultimate state of God realization. Meditation is the evolutionary shortcut and many people have had the experience of noticing how clear and vivid colors appear after their meditations. As we continue meditating we begin to notice many things we have not noticed or felt before for we are beginning to explore wider and finer ranges of vibrations.

9

Physical Properties
Of Color

RADIANT AND PIGMENT COLORS

COLOR IS INHERENT in light and without light color
ceases to exist. If there is no sunlight or we turn off the light
in a room everything appears black. When the source of light
is removed all colors disappear. The colors that we perceive
are the color rays within white light. In the radiant energy
spectrum this is located between the infrared and ultraviolet
rays. This area is enlarged for clarification but in actuality
forms only a small portion of the spectrum. From left to right
the wave lengths become shorter and carry greater quantities
of energy.

Color rays may be transmitted directly to the eye from a
radiant light source; they may be reflected back to the eyes
from an irradiated surface or they may be absorbed by the irradiated surface. Let us first look at radiant light sources which
are direct color energy.

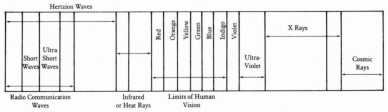

Radiant Energy Spectrum

86

The sun, electric light bulbs, television tubes, a fluorescent watch dial and other luminous bodies are radiant sources of light. In the rainbow the component colors of sunlight are revealed. By the use of filters the component and primary colors of radiant light sources can be discovered. The three primary colors are red, green and purple and are those colors that cannot be produced by mixing other colored lights. When the three light primaries are focused on a single point the result is white light.

Yellow will result when beams of red and green lights are focused on a single point. Red and purple produce mauve, and green and purple produce blue. When two colored light beams are focused on a single point the resulting color is brighter than either of the individual beams. This is an additive color mixture. This is important to remember when using radiant color for healing. Yellow is excellent for problems of constipation when its beam saturates the abdominal region. If we used two light sources, red and green, and focused them on the abdominal region the resulting yellow would be brighter and more potent. In certain cases we may wish to use this combination instead of one beam of yellow.

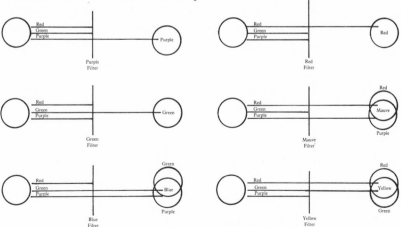

Color Rays Filter Out of White Light

Pigment colors have different properties than radiant colors. As we have seen by adding the color beams of red and green we get yellow. If we do the same thing with pigment colors the result is a dirty grey. The reason is there is no color in the pigment itself but is the result of the color rays from white light being absorbed or reflected by the pigment. A pigment or irradiated surface that reflects all of the color rays of white light appears white. A surface that absorbs all the color rays appears black. A piece of paper that appears green absorbs all of the color rays of white light except green which is reflected back to our eyes. It is the colors that are reflected that give the appearance of color to an irradiated surface. The apparent color of an object is therefore a result of the absorption and reflection properties of a surface. It also depends on the radiant light source. The color perceived from an object in sunlight appears different under a light bulb. The diagram on the opposite page shows that the absorption and reflection of color rays give the impression of color in objects.

Color rays that are absorbed by a material are converted into heat. A dark surface which absorbs all the color rays becomes warmer than a light surface. People in hot climates choose to wear white clothing because they reflect the color rays and heat waves and are therefore cooler.

We can produce colors by mixing two or more pigments together. As in the case for colored lights the three pigment primaries are those which cannot be produced by mixing other pigment colors together. They are red, yellow, and blue. From these three primaries we can produce the other colors of the spectrum. When two primary colors are mixed they produce secondary colors. The secondary colors are: orange (produced by red and yellow), green (produced by yellow and blue), purple (produced by blue and red).

The primary and secondary colors are located on the color wheel by triangles.

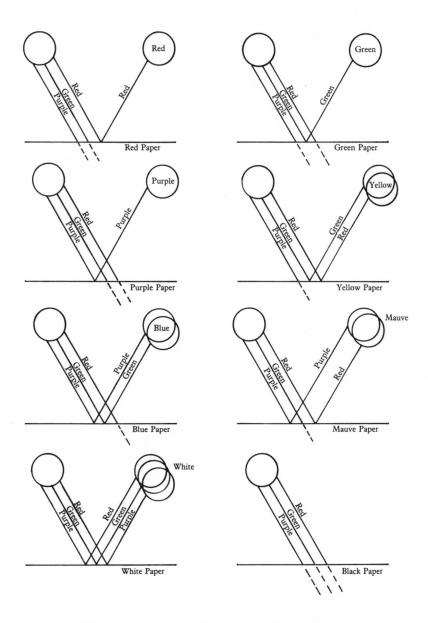

Absorption and Reflection of Color Rays

If we start with red and move clockwise around the circle we will find the spectrum of colors going from longer to shorter wave lengths. Colors directly opposite each other on the color wheel are complementary colors. For example the complement of red is green, red-orange is blue-green and orange is blue and so on. When two primary colors are mixed, the result is the complement of the remaining primary. Red and yellow produces orange which is the complement of the remaining primary blue. When any two complementary colors or the three pigment primaries are mixed the result is blackish grey.

Tertiary colors are those that are produced by mixing the secondary colors. They are: mustard (produced by orange and

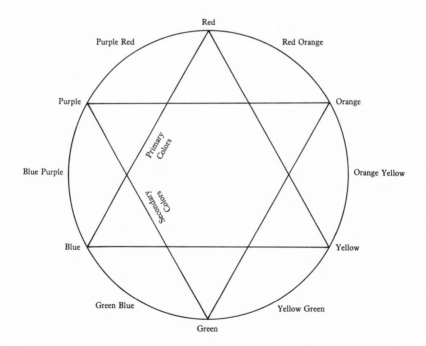

green), olive (produced by green and purple) and russet (produced by purple and orange).

Each pigment absorbs a certain amount of light; therefore, the color resulting from a mixture of two pigments reflects less light than either of its ingredients. Adding pigments together results in a subtraction of light and is known as a subtractive color mixture.

No pigment color reflects exactly the pure color of light. The red pigment reflects not only most of the red light waves, but also some of the orange. The yellow pigment in turn reflects most of the yellow light waves plus some of the orange. When the two pigments are mixed, the red pigment absorbs the yellow light waves. The yellow pigment absorbs the red light waves. Both reflect some of the orange light rays so orange is perceived. The amount of orange absorbed or reflected determines the shade of orange.

No pigment can equal the splendour of nature's colors, the strength and brilliance of colored lights, or the purity of sunlight. When light strikes white paint the rays are partly absorbed by the surface before they are reflected to our eye. Sunlight reaches the eye directly, undiluted in its brilliance and beauty.

COLOR TERMINOLOGY

The term hue refers to a definite wavelength or frequency of the color spectrum. It is the quality by which one color is distinguished from another. Red and yellow are different hues and when they are combined together as they are in pigments, a new hue of orange is created.

Color value or brightness is the quality by which a light color can be distinguished from a dark one. White has the highest color value and black is the lowest. All other colors are positioned between white and black on the brightness scale. Next to white, yellow is the color with the highest value. Purple is the darkest hue next to black.

Color intensity refers to the degree of black contained within a hue. A pure hue that has no black has the highest intensity and as the black increases the intensity of the color is diminished.

Pastels are those colors that contain large amounts of white.

Tints are colors that contain white.

Tones are colors that contain grey.

Shades are colors that contain black.

COLOR CHARACTERISTICS AND RELATIONSHIPS

- Red, orange and yellow are warm, advancing colors. They attract the eye because their energy seems to move toward us. They are best used as highlight colors as they tend to appear more prominent. They also have a tendency to increase the apparent size of an object, especially when the colors are lighter.

- Blue, indigo and violet are cool, receding colors. Their energy is expansive and appears to move away from us. They are best used as background colors. They tend to make objects appear smaller and heavier in weight, especially when the shades are darker.

- Depth is created in a landscape by using receding colors in the background and advancing colors in the foreground.

- Red, orange and yellow are more likely to irritate than green, blue, indigo and violet.

- Colors have two distinguishing characteristics—lustre and image. Lustre colors are radiantly active, whereas image colors are not active of themselves, but hold a given form. Active, luster colors are red, yellow and blue; image colors are peach-blossom, green, black and white.

- Tests have shown that blue has the greatest remembrance value.

- Poor color schemes in dress and environment can lead to fatigue.

- The eye can be shocked by colors if they are too intense.

- Colors that stimulate the appetite are red, warm brown, peach, buff and clear green.

- In studies it is found that pink, pale yellow, lavender and green associate very closely with scents and odors. These are the colors that can best be used to advertise perfumes, flowers or soap.

- The intensity of a color is reduced by adding its complementary hue. If two neighboring shades on the color wheel are mixed the intensity remains high but adding its complement results in a color of little intensity.

- Browns and greys are colors greatly reduced in intensity.

- Adding white increases value or brightness and reduces intensity.

- Adding black reduces value or brightness as well as intensity.

- Rough surfaces tend to dull intensity through absorption. Smooth surfaces which reflect more light rays increase color intensity.

- Simultaneous contrast is the tendency of a color to throw its complementary color into surrounding areas. The shadows on green grass are a result of simultaneous contrast. Red, the complement of green, is thrown into the shadows and gives them a darker appearance. The shadows on a face are the result of the complements of the flesh colors—orange and yellow—being reflected into the shadows. In this case it would be blue and purple.

If two complementary pigment colors of the same intensity are placed together, each will intensify the other. If we place red and green together, the red intensifies green and green does so for red. Red would throw its complement—green—into the green area and green would intensify red by throwing its complement—red—into the red area. The result will be that each color will compete for attention with equal force, resulting in a dancing or vibrating effect along the edge where the two colors meet. To overcome this effect the intensity of red or green can be lowered so they are not competing for attention. The red and green can also be separated by white, black or neutral grey.

- A contrast of colors is used where variety, excitement or emphasizing important details is desired.

- A contrast of colors should be avoided when calm, peace, and receding color effects are needed.

- Background and adjacent colors can change the apparent hue of a color.

- A color can appear more intense and bright by placing it next to its complement or by surrounding it with neutral gray.

- All colors look brighter against a black background or against their complementary colors.

- Colors appear darker on a light background and lighter on a dark background.

- Pale colors are more intensive on a neutral background and less intense on a colorful one.

- The three primaries do not contain any color in common and are therefore not in harmony with each other. If all three primaries are used at full intensity the result will be disharmony. If one primary color were used as the dominant color and mixed with the other primaries, then a harmonious color scheme could result.

- If several bright, pure colors are placed close together they tend to cancel each other out.

- Brilliance can be achieved by the contrast of large areas of neutralized color and a few areas of intense color.

- A monochromatic color scheme uses one dominant color and other colors that contain the dominant. Neighboring colors on the color wheel that have the dominant color give a color scheme that is predominantly warm or cool. It is harmonious, never bold or startling and can be varied a great deal in intensity and value. For example, yellow could be the dominant color and the following colors can be used with it: pale yellow, yellow-orange, yellow-green, cream or lime.

- In the scale of color value or brightness, red is darker than orange, orange is darker than yellow, yellow is lighter than green, green is lighter than blue and blue is lighter than purple. To create harmony when using two colors the above relationship should be kept in mind. If the order is reversed one color has the tendency to look washed out and the other dark and muddy. The result is a disharmony or discord. For example using a green that is darker than blue results in the blue appearing weak and ineffective and the green heavy.

- When using two or more colors it is important to let one color dominate the others. It is best not to use all colors at equal value and intensity in areas of equal size. Areas of high intensity should be smaller than subdued areas to produce a good balance.

- To obtain a cool color by mixing two other colors, select the coolest hues that will produce the desired color. Use the warmest hues when trying to obtain a warm color.

- The best light source when matching colors is natural daylight. North light is preferable to direct sunlight, which produces too much glare.

- Most artificial lighting is deficient in some light rays of the spectrum. A color will look different in sunlight than under artificial light. When matching colors it is important to be consistent and use the same light source.

- When mixing pale colors it is advisable to add the color to white in very small quantities until the desired color is achieved.

- Dark tones are best lightened by adding the lighter color to the darker one in small amounts until the proper shade is found.

- Let a color dry before checking a color match. Pigment colors look different when wet than they do when dry.

COLOR RESPONSE

Color causes an emotional response. It affects us consciously and subconsciously; therefore, our response to color is impulsive and also a product of training or tradition. Certain colors represent certain emotions, activities or traits of character. Colors are warm or cold, relaxing or exciting, bright or depressing, pleasing or irritating.

The American flag is an excellent example of color symbolism. The Continental Congress defined the color symbology thus: "White for purity and innocence; red for hardiness and valor; blue for vigilance, perseverance and justice."

Dr. Carl Jung states that there are four kinds of basic human inner experiences. Most people associate particular colors with each of the four experiences. Red is connected with emotion; yellow with association of different experiences; green with sensations, or reaction to experiences; and blue with reasoning.

From the above association of experiences with color we can, for example, plan the color scheme in our home. First decide what kind of experience is most common for each room. Once that is established, then the color that relates to that experience will be the logical one to use. In the kitchen the main experience is the sensation of taste. Green is associated with sensation and can be used very effectively. Green also is calm and cooling and would afford a good atmosphere for eating.

COLOR PREFERENCE

In color planning, individuality is a key factor. Each color has an innate quality and a universal, humanitarian response. Because color association and conditioning are linked with dramatic life experiences, certain colors may affect an individual uniquely. When working with color keep in mind its characteristics, but also inwardly feel how you respond to these colors or combinations of colors. Use the ones that work best for you.

Tests have shown that sex and age have definite effects on color selection. Children are attracted to bright, sharp colors. Their perception is limited to strong, intense colors of red, yellow, green and blue. Dark shades and pastels have little attraction for children. Adults prefer a greater variety of colors than children, due to a more developed color perception.

Studies show that red was the favorite color of women whereas men chose blue. Men preferred strong colors for their surroundings, while women chose softer pastel colors.

COLOR SCHEMES IN THE HOME

Surrounding ourselves with harmonious colors in our environment uplifts us and keeps us positive and joyous. Following certain concepts in home decor will lead to an improved living environment.

Three colors are sufficient for a single room. A color can be repeated by changing the intensity, value, and texture to avoid monotony. Dashes of a single, bright color can be used for the highlights when three colors are used. This gives the room a feeling of unity, harmony and purpose.

If a restful room is desired a color scheme using the blue end of the spectrum would be beneficial. An exciting room can be achieved by using the red end of the spectrum, and also bright complementary color schemes with bold contrasts.

When complementary colors are used they provide both warmth and coolness. They should, however, be toned down in order to prevent strong contrast so as to make the room restful and livable.

Chilly rooms with a northern exposure are enhanced by the use of warm color schemes to make them cheery and inviting. Sunny rooms are better served by a cool color scheme.

In home decoration there needs to be contrasts of dark and light as well as dull and bright. The largest areas—walls and floors—should be considered first. Floors are usually kept dull or dark and walls can be light or dark. The colors for furniture, drapery, slipcovers and other accessories can be light or dark, bright or dull.

COLOR IN INDUSTRY

Proper color schemes give various advantages in advertising.

- They can identify a company and product.

- The proper use of color can attract buyers and increase sales.

- A greater value can be given to the product in the customer's eyes.

Proper color schemes and lighting are very important in factories and offices. They can:

Reduce nervous tension and eyestrain.
Increase worker efficiency and morale.
Most important of all, lower accident rates.

Eye fatigue comes from inadequate lighting, glare, extreme contrasts between work and background, or prolonged concentration on a work area with no means for resting the eyes occasionally. A dark desk top, for example, causes contrast with white paper. This problem can be avoided by a light or grey desk top which will cut down the contrast and be more restful to the eyes. Restful background colors are helpful where there is intense concentration on a work area. Neutral gray backgrounds eliminate visual distractions from the field of vision and help keep concentration centered on the work. Dazzling white walls and ceiling can produce eyestrain if sunlight shines on them with full intensity. Light-colored walls can reduce glare and still give good light reflection.

Highly visible colors can be used to help the eye register quickly on moving parts of machinery and thus reduce accidents. Machinery can be color coded to indicate lubrication points and painted in various shades to make them more appealing to work with. Color can provide a contrast between working material and the machinery itself and thus reduce rejects and accidents.

The use of color in printing attracts the eye and makes reading more pleasant. Everyone enjoys color in a book. Black print and white paper can become very boring after a short period of time. It should be remembered that print in light colors seems smaller than the same size in darker letters. Light colors blend together if too closely spaced, resulting in poor legibility. On a long printed page it is best to use a pale tint for the paper. A bright color would be too tiring for the eyes and would decrease legibility.

Bright colors are used for farm machinery, school buses, fire trucks and so on for greater visibility. Light, chrome yellow is used for school buses because of its high visibility in daylight and under headlights at night. It contrasts strongly with highway white or black and the blue of the sky. The exact shade has been standardized in the Manual on Uniform Traffic Control Services for Streets and Highways published by the American Association of State Highway Officials.

COLOR IN THE WARDROBE

Often people wear colors that are fashionable and do not consider what is best for them. Some general helpful hints are as follows:

- White or light clothing reflects more light to the face than darker colors.

- Those with dark complexion and hair would do well to wear off-whites, cream and ivory.

- Black tends to make a person look thinner. White, pale colors and large, brightly-colored prints tend to make one look stouter.

- Bright red hair goes well with contrasting darker colors. Dark red hair blends best with lighter shades. Pale blue-greens and blue-purples are good choices in color. Bright reds and magenta would, however, make one's hair look rusty.

- Dark brunette hair is enhanced by muted colors—strong blue and light, warm yellows.

- Medium brown hair goes well with most colors. Rich warm orange, cardinal red and guardsmen blue are excellent choices.

- People with blond hair should avoid bright yellows and tans close to the hue of their hair as it will make it look washed out. Pastels, magenta and blues are good colors to use.

- People with an olive complexion do best to avoid certain shades of green as it makes the skin appear muddy. Pale peach, beige or creamy white enhances an olive complexion.

- Pastels, yellows and muddy colors are best avoided by those who have aging, yellow skin. Sapphire, emerald, amethyst or deep ruby would be good choices.

HEALING PROPERTIES OF THE SPECTRUM OF PHYSICAL COLORS

The rainbow or the spectrum of colors we see are rays passing through a prism containing seven colors. At the lower end of the spectrum the red, orange and yellow have similar properties. They are the stimulating, vitalizing vibrations. They have the ability to dilate and expand and are also warming and increase body heat. From these properties we can see that if a person were bathed with red light he would absorb the influence of the red vibration into his organism. If we observed the circulation system we would see that the blood becomes stimulated and the blood vessels dilate and expand, reddening the skin. By knowing the effect of red on the body we can use it to our advantage. If in certain diseases we want to increase the blood flow to help remove mucous and toxins from the body we would use red. If, however, we use too much red for too long, the toxins may race throughout the body too quickly and the body may not be able to counteract them fast enough. This could result in a condition worse than the original problem was in the first place, so each color should be used with respect and sensitivity. Red, orange and yellow are alkaline in effect and are non-electric and magnetic. If one wishes to neutralize the acid of heavy proteins in one's diet, then alkaline foods should be used that vibrate to the colors of red, orange and yellow.

Healing Properties of Color

Color		Properties
	Yang	
Red		—stimulating
Orange		—vitalizing
		—warming
Yellow		—dilates
		—promotes body heat
		—alkaline
		—non-electric
		—magnetic
Green	*Neutral*	—Neutral color; balance point in the spectrum
	Yin	
Blue		—restrictor
		—astringent
Indigo		—cooling
		—contractor
Violet		—lowers body heat
		—acidic
		—non-magnetic
		—electric

Green is mid-point in the spectrum and separates the three color vibrations above from the three below. It is therefore the neutral color or balance point in the spectrum. It is neither acid nor alkaline. The green vibration is at the mid-point between the hot, activating red and the cool, constricting blue ends of the spectrum. Cosmic Intelligence has created the wonders of nature with green predominating. Green is a physically relaxing color. When we go to the country and draw the vibration of green into our bodies, our nervous system becomes relaxed and calm. If God had created nature with red predominating we might be mental and physical wrecks. We would constantly be over-stimulated by the red entering our eyes and affecting the pituitary.

In effect we stimulate the whole body by perceiving color because the pituitary is the master gland that controls the other endocrine glands and their hormone secretions. If we constantly absorbed red we would be continually restless and ever on the move. Through the understanding of this principle we can see that it is advisable not to wear tinted sunglasses because the color vibration will have a powerful effect on consciousness. By eating too many red foods instead of greens we end up running around in circles, irritable and violent with each other. Green is the balance point between Yin and Yang; red, orange, yellow are Yang; blue, indigo, and violet are Yin.

The vibrational properties of blue, indigo and violet are the opposite of red, orange and yellow. They have cooling, antiseptic properties and are electric and constrictive. Blue, indigo and violet are also acidic, electric, and non-magnetic in nature. If we take the example of the circulatory system, we can see that these colors restrict or contract the blood vessels. This is helpful to know if there is excess bleeding and we want to help in clotting the blood. Indigo light, for example, bathed on the area aids in clotting. On the other hand, if we were to use too much indigo for too long then the over-constriction could cause the blood pressure to go up. If it goes up too far, there can be unnecessary complications.

From these properties we can see that the blue end of the spectrum is excellent for burns as it has the ability to send the blood inward reducing heat and easing pain and inflamed conditions. We would not give a person who is melancholy and depressed treatment from the blue end of the spectrum, however, for he needs the stimulating colors. Blue is for those who are over-agitated and need the calming, relaxing benefit of these colors. Sensitivity is the key word when using color for healing. The characteristics of the colors must be known and applied with respect.

Researchers have shown that the electrons of a metal plate react to spectral wavelengths. When a beam of violet light falls upon a metal plate, a shower of electrons at a specific velocity is ejected by the plate. If a lower frequency color such as red were used, the velocity of the electrons emitted would be lowered. It is the color and not its intensity that affects the velocity of the electrons from the plate. If the intensity of the color were diminished, it would result in fewer electrons being emitted, but the velocity would remain the same. Einstein explains that the photons of the violet light (the higher regions of the spectrum) carry more energy than the photons of red (the lower regions of the spectrum). The velocity in which the electron is ejected from the plate is then directly proportional to the energy of the photon striking it. Color frequencies move matter. As the electrons in a metal plate are affected by color, so our bodily system is similarly affected.

If we understand certain bodily principles we can use color very effectively and beneficially in healing. Color inhibits or stimulates each organ or system. Anabolism is a constructive, building-up process. It is a function of constructive metabolism by which food is changed into living tissue. Catabolism is the opposite and is a process in which living tissue is changed into waste products of a simpler chemical composition. It is, therefore, destructive metabolism. By this we can see how color can affect the metabolic rate in man. Anabolism is a function of the red Yang end of the spectrum and catabolism is a function of the blue Yin end of the spectrum. Red activates the liver which aids in production of red blood cells. Violet, on the other hand, stimulates the spleen which functions to destroy wornout blood cells and produce white ones and phagocytes which destroy harmful bacteria. If we use green, it affects the pituitary which regulates metabolism by bringing a balance between the liver and spleen.

By knowing the color equivalent of certain elements or compounds we can bring about healing in the body. Fever results from an over-production of hydrogen, which is red, and carbon, which is yellow. By using blue, which is the color of oxygen, we are able to neutralize the excess hydrogen and carbon. Oxygen combines with hydrogen to produce water and will be excreted through the breath, skin and kidneys. Oxygen combines with carbon to produce carbon dioxide, which is removed through the lungs in respiration.

Let us look at the vibration of orange. Orange is the color of calcium and by using it we can overcome and aid many problems of the bones. By an understanding of the principles of color we can see the tremendous benefit and potential they possess for the healing arts.

It should be remembered that color enters the body through various channels. We take in light and color through our aura and chakra centers. The color rays from the sun are absorbed by the etheric body and distributed via the spleen chakra to the other spinal centers and to the physical body. The eyes receive color vibrations, as does the skin. When color is absorbed through the skin it affects all the other systems of the body through the circulation and nervous system. When taking in color on one location, our body transmits it to affect the entire organism. It is very important to remember this when we are using chemicals on our skin or hair for these ingredients will affect our entire being. Even a very mild stimulus of toxic materials over a long period of time can produce serious disease.

Color is a vibration and has its own intelligence. It knows its work in all phases of existence. Colors work independently and together. Negative reactions in our emotions, thoughts and our physical, astral and other bodies can be the result of color starvation or excess on any level of our being—physical, mental, or spiritual. In the case of color starvation, we need to introduce the needed color into our system.

If an organ is clogged and requires stimulation, the proper color needs to be administered to bring the organ back to its proper vibrating frequency. If a certain color energy is in excess, then the opposite, or color of affinity, is required to neutralize and restore balance.

Red has an affinity with blue, orange with indigo, yellow with violet, lemon with turquoise, scarlet with purple. Color is a tool that can help to bring about the proper realignment and resonance of vibrations within our being so that we can live a perfect and balanced existence. To bring ourselves to a point of balance and harmony and become perfect citizens of the cosmos we must vibrate in tune with the natural rhythm of all the colors of the physical, mental and spiritual planes of existence.

INDIVIDUAL COLOR PROPENSITIES

A Red Environment

The vibration of red is one of excitation, stimulation and warmth. Red can be used very effectively in places where people are suffering from lack of initiative or melancholy or if they have lost the desire to live. A predominantly red environment can help stimulate the will and life force to overcome depression and bring about positive changes in one's life. In environments where physical exercise is the focus, the vital and stimulating properties of red can be of great benefit. It is a tremendous asset in weight-lifting training rooms where great strength and vitality are required.

Since red is highly stimulating it ought to be avoided in places where rest and calm are being fostered. Too much red in one's bedroom not only increases the passions, but likely would tend to make one restless and agitated, resulting in disturbed and unsatisfying sleep. Red should also be avoided in areas of concentration, such as study and meditation rooms. Too great an exposure to its vibration will cause thoughts to become agitated and restless. Red is not to be used in eating areas, for its irritating quality will cause people to eat in a hurry and not digest food properly.

Red stimulates people to action and it is well to avoid in areas where people are prone to suicide. Red should not be used in areas where a great deal of precision work is required and where haste in a project would result in an accident. Use it with caution and respect because of its reactive and impulsive effects. Red energy rushes toward us. It arrests, and focuses attention; therefore, it is best used as a highlight color. Orange and yellow are also good as highlight colors.

Red in the Wardrobe

Red socks and underwear are good in the winter, because its energy offers tremendous warmth to help overcome inner chills. Using a red jogging suit for running and exercise is very helpful. It emanates a vibration of vitality and strength. Extroverts who want to proclaim their presence will often wear very loud red shades. People who feel aggressive and are looking for a fight may subconsciously choose red. We knowingly or subconsciously choose the clothes we wear according to our inner moods. By knowing the psychology of color we can choose a light, calming blue to help us counteract our aggressive times. Red is a passionate color, too, and by wearing hot red colors we may project this image. If we want to jump around like a monkey during our sleep, we might try sleeping in red pajamas.

The Healing Properties of Red

Red controls the coccygeal center at the base of the spine. This vibration manifesting through the coccygeal center governs the vitality of the physical body, especially the creative, procreative, restorative process along with the lower limbs. Red is an energizer and stimulates the nervous system, circulation, cerebrospinal fluid and the senses. Since it energizes the senses, red is very beneficial in deficiencies of smell, sight, hearing, taste and touch.

Its warming qualities make it excellent for chronic chills and colds. Red especially energizes the liver and activates the adrenals. Stimulating the coccygeal center with red will result in adrenalin being released into the blood stream. The release of adrenalin may help overcome the psychological problems of fear and assist one to take action and overcome the fear.

Red is very helpful in removing dormant or sluggish conditions. It also clears congestion and mucous from the body through its activating, dilating qualities. It increases the red blood corpuscles, hemoglobin and iron count. The red energy has the ability to stimulate the manufacture of iron. The vibration of red decomposes the ferric salt crystals in the body and splits them into their component parts of iron and salt. The iron can then be used by the red blood cells. The liver stores the iron of hemoglobin and when it is activated by the red it will release hemoglobin iron molecules. These molecules are then used by the red blood cells to transport oxygen to all parts of the body to carry on growth. Feelings of tiredness and inertia can be alleviated by the use of this color.

Red should not be used for emotionally disturbed people, inflammatory conditions or for those who are easily irritated. It ought never be used alone in treatments, but needs to be followed with green or blue for a few moments to bring one back into balance.

An Orange Environment

Orange is a social color and can be used very effectively in community centers and other meeting places. In the home it is best used in rooms where the family members gather and where guests are received and entertained. The energy of orange is a mixture of the vitalizing physical red element and the intellectual yellow. Orange is considered the wisdom ray, the ray of ideas. Orange is very beneficial when placed in areas of creative study. The vibration of courage and optimism is crystalized in the orange hue. The energy of orange is excellent for hospital rooms. It can be used in intensive care units where its qualities are important in helping the patient recover and get well. It is also excellent in pre-operating rooms to help the patient become saturated with optimistic confidence and to overcome fears. The color stimulates the appetite and can be used where this is needed. Orange is a highlight color and so should be used in moderation. If there is an overabundance of orange, it may result in overbearing feelings and even lead to a tendency to overindulge.

Orange in the Wardrobe

Whenever consciously or subconsciously we choose to wear orange, a feeling of courage and optimism is probably bubbling within us. If this quality is missing in our life, we should definitely bring orange into our wardrobe. Orange is a social color and will help us to feel a deeper interest and concern for others and a desire to be in their presence. If we feel an underlying fear of meeting and mixing with people we should put ourselves in orange robes of courage.

If we overdo this hue in our wardrobe, however, we may feel and appear like a social butterfly flitting everywhere. We may even become too dependent on others and fail to use our own initiative. Many monastic orders of the east wear orange-colored robes. Orange is a symbol of finite creation returning to the infinite. In the beauty of autumn we behold the leaves and fields taking on an orange tinge.

The Healing Properties of Orange

Orange controls the sacral chakra and also the spleen. Manifesting through the sacral chakra orange aids in circulatory, assimilative and distributive processes. It releases energy when applied to the spleen. Orange rules the abdominal area and if one is having problems with this area and cannot eliminate properly it is often due to a psychological tendency to cling to the past. If we find we are not rising above old thoughts and bad habits and are holding onto undesirable attitudes, then problems are likely to take their toll in the abdominal region. Treat this region with orange via the sacral chakra. It is a lung builder and respiratory stimulant and therefore is beneficial for lung problems. Orange carries the potency of both copper and calcium.

The heating qualities of orange help to remove cramps and muscle spasms. If there is abnormal putrefaction in the stomach, orange has been known to induce vomiting to clear the unsuitable matter. It will also relieve gas in the digestive tract. Orange is the color of calcium and is used to aid in the development of bones and to correct bone softness. Orange provides physical energy, a powerful tonic, and it is also a mental stimulus. It is a combination of red and yellow, therefore it blends the physical elements of red with the intellectual element of yellow.

A Yellow Environment

Yellow is the manifestation of the mental, creative vibration. Its use is beneficial in libraries and study rooms. The Sunshine School of York, England found that retarded children learned more readily in a yellow classroom. In order to channel the concentrated energy to a higher manifestation, blue or violet can be used with yellow to counteract the overstimulating effect of yellow. Yellow energy is one of Joy and its shining, joyous vibration moves toward us so we will do well to utilize it whenever possible.

Yellow in the Wardrobe

The sunshine quality of this color emphasizes the joy of living and when we wear it we shower this vibration on ourselves and others. Whenever we feel depressed, wearing yellow will uplift our spirits. It is also the mental vibration and wearing it will give an added security to our intellectual abilities. Too much yellow, however, may give the impression that we are robots of reason and devoid of feeling. It may also make us appear too critical and resemble a Mr. Smart type of personality.

The Healing Properties of Yellow

Yellow activates the lumbar or solar plexus center and controls digestive processes in the stomach. It aids in digestion and increases bowel movements; therefore it is very good for indigestion and constipation. This vibration is used to stimulate the pancreas and intestines and the production of digestive fluids such as bile and hydrochloric acid. Natural laxatives contain the yellow vibration—for example senna root, prunes and figs.

The solar plexus is known as the second brain of the nervous system. Yellow is a motor nerve stimulant which energizes the muscles. It is a nerve builder as well for the sensory and motor nervous systems. Yellow is good for mental and nervous exhaustion and depression. Its action on the liver, intestines and skin is stimulating, cleansing and eliminative. It therefore helps to purify the bodily system.

Yellow generally improves the texture of the skin. It cleanses the body's pores which then secrete unwanted material through sweating. The energy of yellow is used to aid in liver trouble.

If life does not seem secure, we feel anger and frustration. When we find we are having trouble making decisions, this will add to our frustration and insecurity. If these psychological problems bring the emotions of anger and frustration, this will be held in the liver and will cause problems in its physical functioning. Using yellow aids in the healing of the liver. Regular treatments will be needed until the positive vibrations of security and assimilation are manifesting clearly again.

Yellow has the ability to activate the lymphatic system. The energy of yellow is used to expel worms and parasites and is a spleen depressant. Yellow should never be used if one is suffering from acute inflammation, fever, delirium, diarrhea, overexcitement or palpitations of the heart.

A Green Environment

The green vibration is one of serene, calming peace and is best used in areas that are set aside for rest and relaxation. Divine Intelligence has made the green color predominate in His creative environment of nature. It is best to follow this example and take advantage of the tranquility of green. The bedroom is an ideal place to use green as it calms away tensions and anxieties and aids peaceful sleep. Since green is the color of healing, its use is very beneficial in hospital rooms where healing and growth are required. The Green Ray rules the heart and the color bestows feelings of brotherly love. Green's vibration of harmony and brotherhood make it an excellent color to be used in rooms where political and world affairs are discussed and initiated.

Green in the Wardrobe

Green is at the center of the spectrum. It separates the three stimulating colors below from the three calming colors above. It therefore brings balance and harmony. If we wear green we appear and feel stable and secure. It makes us aware that we are able to balance the spiritual and material ways of life by keeping our heads in the clouds while our feet are firmly planted on the ground. Too much green, however, may make us appear rigid and fixed in our ways. It is the color of healing and can effectively be worn by both nurses and doctors. Patients would feel the healing benefit if they wore this color. Green is soothing to the nerves and body and wearing green pajamas can help one achieve a peaceful sleep. When just relaxing, relax with green.

The Healing Properties of Green

Green stimulates and activates the dorsal or heart chakra. It is a tonic to the body because it relaxes the nervous system and induces calmness. It is also considered a sedative to help one relax and sleep. It is extremely beneficial in cases of irritability and exhaustion. Green is a pituitary stimulant, emotional builder. Green stimulates the rebuilding of muscles and tissue. It is the color of nitrogen which makes up the largest percentage of the atmosphere. Amino acids—which are the building blocks of proteins—depend to a great extent on the element nitrogen. It has antiseptic qualities which aid in destroying germs and bacteria and so preventing decay in the body.

The energy of green is helpful in all problems of the heart. The inability to love because of a deep hurt, experienced in this life or the past, can be aided by it. Green also aids the etheric body of man by loosening and equalizing it.

A Blue Environment

Blue is excellent for the bedroom as its tranquil vibration calms the mind and leads to a peaceful sleep. The combination of blue and green is a very good one for bedrooms because the blue element relaxes the mind and green the physical. If too much blue is used in a room other than the bedroom and is not broken up by some other color it will make one sleepy. If we are not careful, it could put us in a blue mood as well.

Blue is also cooling. A large corporation manager decided to paint the office walls a cool, blue-green color to rest the eyes of the stenographers. He found that the girls caught colds, and absenteeism increased. The temperature remained the same, but the psychological effect was one of chilliness. The manager overcame this problem by painting the backs of the stenographers' chairs a bright warm orange. The women began to take off their sweaters under the warming influence of the orange. Soon complaints stopped and things were back to normal.

Blue is an expansive color and whenever there is a need to make a room seem larger blue can be used. It seems to draw us out of ourselves into a larger world. It has an elusive, drawing quality that pulls us, but as we try to approach it, it always seems to move further away. Violet, indigo and blue transfer feelings of spaciousness and seem to retreat from us. Their use in color decor is best as background colors.

The blue end of the spectrum has a softer vibration in comparison to the aggressive red end. Blue's vastness and tranquility expands us, helping us transcend all petty worries and anxieties. In meditation and contemplation areas, blue, indigo and violet are excellent colors to use because of their spiritual qualities. The energy of the blue end causes a person to go within himself, whereas the red end tends to make one become more extroverted.

Blue in the Wardrobe

The person who wears blue appears calm and tranquil. Whenever we feel restless energy we can counteract this with a blue garment. Blue pajamas and bedspreads aid in giving a night of rest. Blue is also an antiseptic color and can be used effectively in all areas where cleanliness is a must. Blue clothing for doctors and janitors utilizes this quality. Blue is an expansive, spiritual color and sings of the freedom of the soul. When wearing blue we tend to feel the need for freedom of creative expression and might also rebel against rigid standards and forms. When we wish to create, we would do well to bring the creative color of blue into our wardrobe.

The Healing Properties of Blue

Blue controls the cervical or throat which is the center of creativity in man. The voice is the greatest vehicle of self expression. Blue is beneficial for all throat and speech problems. If one has trouble telling the truth and is not honest in life, then throat problems tend to result. If we find ourselves worried too much over nonessentials and preoccupied with petty details, then the throat will suffer as well. Blue is the vibration of truth and when the throat chakra is bathed with it, it will aid in developing this quality.

Blue reduces fever or inflammations and returns the blood stream to normal when the body becomes inflamed and overactive. The combination of the blue oxygen, red hydrogen and yellow carbon produces water (H_2O) and carbon dioxide (CO_2), respectively. Perspiration is the result of these chemical reactions, automatically reducing fever. The energy of blue checks irritation from itching and stings and is excellent for burns, cuts and bruises on the skin. Blue encourages perspiration and builds vitality in the body and is also an excellent antiseptic with bacteriocidal properties. It is cooling, electrical and has the property of restricting or contracting.

Blue is a relaxant and soothing to the mind and is excellent for overexcitement and irritation. Green is calming and soothing to the body, whereas blue is soothing to the mind and is very helpful in emotional situations. The blue should not be used, however, if one is suffering from a cold, muscle cramps, paralysis, chronic rheumatism or hypertension.

An Indigo Environment

Indigo represents spiritual perception and intuition. When we work on an intuitive level we can profit by having the indigo vibration in our surroundings. Balance is the keynote of a perfected life. If we find that we are dwelling too much in the non-physical and becoming spaced out, we should remove ourselves from the vibration of indigo and expose ourselves to red. The vibration of red in our environment will tend to root us in the now. If we discover we are becoming too matter-of-fact because of an intellectual yellow energy, we need to turn to the indigo vibration to allow intuition to guide us.

Indigo in the Wardrobe

Indigo is a mystical color and could be used very effectively as a hue to be worn during meditation. The indigo ray denotes the spiritual eye, which is the will center in man. The development of the will in man may express itself in the need for self-expression and identity. Indigo jeans, when they were first introduced, became an expression for individuality and radical tendencies. The moderating tendency of indigo can perhaps help us to remember our highest goals in life, experiencing and expressing our soul individuality and conforming our will to the Will of God.

The Healing Properties of Indigo

Indigo activates the spiritual eye center in the forehead and controls the pineal gland. It mediates the psychic currents of the finer bodies. The energy of indigo is helpful in certain mental disorders. It is a parathyroid stimulant and a thyroid depressant; therefore, it is a respiratory depressor. Its contracting properties arrest discharges, and help reduce or stop excessive bleeding. Indigo aids in the production of phagocytes in the spleen to destroy harmful micro-organisms. It is a purifier of the blood stream and a depressant of milk production in mammals.

Indigo is an excellent anaesthetic which sedates and helps diminish overactivity and excitement. It has properties that could make one totally insensible to pain. Its effect is not hypnotic nor are there any after-effects, but it can raise the consciousness to a higher plane of vibration beyond the awareness of the physical body.

Indigo is cooling and electric in nature. It has an effect on vision, smell and hearing and a beneficial healing effect on all problems of the eyes, nose and ears. If one is continually prejudiced and cannot see situations in life clearly, then eye trouble will probably manifest itself. It aids in resealing the aura to prevent the intrusion of unwanted and negative energies.

A Violet Environment

The vibration of violet symbolizes divine realization and is an excellent color for meditation and contemplation rooms. Leonardo da Vinci said, "The power of meditation can be ten times greater under violet light falling through the stained-glass window of a quiet church." Richard Wagner placed violet curtains in front of himself when he desired to compose high, spiritual music. Violet aids in the development of creative imagination and should be used in children's playrooms and other creative areas.

Violet in the Wardrobe

Violet is desired and worn by those who feel the spiritual essence of life and have a highly creative imagination. It could be worn effectively by anyone who works for God. Unlike the drab tones of black, which represent suffering and sorrow, white and violet bring forth the true spiritual essence. When exploring the vast realms of creative imagination, you can wear a dash of violet to inspire you on your way.

The Healing Properties of Violet

Violet controls the thousand-petaled lotus or the crown chakra at the top of the head. The pituitary gland is the link in the physical body with this thousand-petaled lotus. The energy of violet is a depressant to various organs and systems such as the heart, muscles, lymphatic glands and motor nervous system. Violet promotes the production of leucocytes (white blood cells) and purifies the blood. It also nourishes the blood in the upper brain region.

The violet vibration stimulates the spleen and is good for bone growth. It maintains the potassium-sodium balance in the body. It has the ability to calm the violently insane and control irritability. Its energy has a soothing and tranquilizing effect on the nervous system. To people such as artists, actors and musicians who tend to be nervous and high strung by nature the violet ray helps to restore peace and calm. These imaginative people may not be grounded on the earth in the way others are and when they function here their nervous systems may be shocked by the grosser vibrations of the earth plane.

Scalp diseases are aided by the use of violet. It also can be an aid in controlling excessive hunger. Violet should be used with caution as the photons of violet carry a greater energy quantum than the rest of the spectrum. Average temperaments may find it difficult to adjust to the rapid, vibratory energy of violet.

A White Environment

White is the essence of all colors and where purity is required it is the logical choice. It complements all colors and adds to the essence of the one it is placed beside. When white is added to a color, it becomes imbued with greater spiritual qualities. If the shade has a greater content of black, then the color represents negative qualities. Dark, dingy yellow indicates jealousy and suspicion, whereas golden yellow is the Christ Ray of high soul attributes. The pastel shades represent greater spiritual qualities. The clearer and brighter the shade, the greater are the positive qualities.

White reflects heat and color rays. White ocean liners are used on tropical cruises to keep the passengers cool and comfortable. Interstate buses and transport aircraft use white or aluminum roofs to provide greater comfort for passengers in the summertime. White is used effectively in buildings and homes in extremely hot climates.

White in the Wardrobe

White universally represents purity and when we feel our morality slipping we would do well to surround ourselves with this vibration. White represents the sum total of all colors and therefore is the sum total. When we feel and want to manifest perfection of soul the vibration of white is the one to wear.

The Healing Properties of White Light

The pure White Light of Spirit contains all the Cosmic Rays and therefore contains all the qualities of each individual ray. The same is true of sunlight. It is the sum total of all the colors on the planet earth and therefore has all the qualities of the colors within itself. By taking in the pure energy of sunlight we can recharge our bodies with all the colors and imbibe all of the healing qualities at once. It is important to try to bathe ourselves in the sun's healing rays every day. By following this practice we can gain tremendous energy and vitalizing power. People in cities are often confined to artificial environments with electric lighting and electronic devices. These tend to deplete energy and make one feel irritable and uncomfortable. Energies become concentrated in the lower end of the spectrum and so are distorted.

We must make the effort to get out in the sun even if it is only for a short time every day. Of course we need to avoid over-exposing ourselves to the point where the skin burns. To overdo it and get a sunburn makes the effect worse than not getting any sun at all. If we concentrate on receiving the sun's rays and feeling its vitalizing power energizing us, we will know when we've had enough and so receive greater benefit. Feel and visualize the sun tanning your skin and its rays penetrating deep within, saturating every organ and cell. If we mentally see the rays saturating any diseased area, the healing energy will be intensified and the healing quickened.

The Properties of Ultraviolet

Ultraviolet energy has bacteriological properties which guard the body against disease. Ultraviolet is important in calcium-phosphorus metabolism. This vibration acts as a sedative to pain and is good for the heart and lungs. It stimulates the action of the sympathetic system.

The Properties of Magenta

The energy of magenta is a combination of red and violet. It is an aura builder and emotional stabilizer. Magenta has diuretic properties. Magenta will help to bring the adrenals, heart and circulatory system to a state of equilibrium.

The Properties of Purple

Purple is a mixture of red and blue with the blue portion predominant. It is a kidney depressant. The purple vibration induces relaxation and sleep and decreases sensitivity to pain. It lowers the body temperature and thus helps to control fevers. It also acts as a stimulant and increases the activity of the veins.

The Properties of Turquoise

The vibration of turquoise is made up of blue and green. Its energy is excellent as a skin tonic and it rebuilds burned skin. When treating a burn, use the blue energy first to relieve pain, then follow with turquoise to quicken the growth of new skin formation. Turquoise is a brain depressant and is helpful to those who are mentally overactive. The use of turquoise is beneficial in acute conditions.

The Properties of Lemon

The energy of lemon is a mixture of green and yellow. The green in it acts as a cleanser and the yellow as a motor stimulant to throw off unwanted debris. Lemon relieves congestion and brings it to the surface. The lemon vibration is beneficial in the removal of congestion from the kidneys and gall bladder. Clogged sinuses respond well to lemon. Lemon will help to induce coughing when it is necessary to remove mucous and fluids from the air passages and lungs. Phosphorus vibrates to it, so it is therefore an excellent bone builder. Lemon stimulates the manufacture of collagen, an important component of bone structure, vessel walls and other tissues. It is also a stimulant to the brain, thymus and digestive system and has laxative properties. Lemon is beneficial in all chronic conditions.

The Properties of Scarlet

The energy of scarlet is a combination of red and blue with the red being predominent. Scarlet is a kidney stimulant. If kidney problems begin to manifest it is often because we have reached a point in life where we do not feel clear about some important situation. It seems as if our clarity has flown out the window. The energy of scarlet will bathe the kidneys with its transforming vibration.

10

Methods of Treatment

THOUGHT IS ONE of the most potent forces in the universe. God created the entire universe out of His imaginative thought. As children of God we have the potential to create, even as He does. We are the architects of every phase of our lives through our own thoughts and actions. The body temple that our soul is wearing is the result of all our thoughts in this life and those past. If we came into this world with some malfunctioning organ and disease it was because we had created it sometime in the past.

We must take responsibility for our thoughts and actions. No one is to blame for our misfortunes but ourselves. All bodily problems are a result of our negative thoughts, emotions and actions. We have a metaphysical and psychological anatomy. We have created our bodies; our thoughts and actions in this life will determine the body we create in the next. We can create whatever we wish; if we want to improve our destiny, it is within our power at each and every moment.

All healing from an outside source such as medicine and drugs is limited compared to the power of consciousness. Color treatments are finer and more direct than medicine for they are direct energy. Color rays are vibration close to the source. When one receives a color treatment this energy causes certain chemical reactions in the body which stimulate the healing process. If one is not attentive to what is going on during treatments and allows his thoughts to roam, the healing effect will be minimized. If after the treatment one goes home to watch violent movies and continues to carry on in negative pastimes, then the good effect of the treatment will be cancelled out.

When we use the mind directly and visualize color, then we make the connection of understanding we ourselves are responsible for the healing and no one else. When we tune in with our own strength then we grow physically, mentally and spiritually. By using color coupled with mind power we are able to use this enhanced power to overcome bad habits which are the cause of disease in the first place.

Paramahansa Yogananda used to give divine healings when he first started his mission, but discontinued after some time. He then solely dedicated all of his attention to helping others to know God and purify their own consciousnesses. He realized that people would just go back to their old negative life styles and the same problems would in time manifest themselves again and they would be back for another healing. He dedicated his full attention to helping people see the quirks in their own natures that were causing the diseases in the first place.

Most inharmonies in the body are a result of negative thinking, feeling, action and spiritual ignorance of one's soul and God. By realizing this and purifying our natures we can be free of physical problems. Working with one's thoughts is the most effective way possible for it gives us the power to develop consciousness and change our lives.

MEDITATION ON THE WHITE LIGHT

The White Light of Spirit has the cosmos within it. It contains every vitamin, mineral, medicine and color. The Divine White Light is the sum total of all vibrations, all the wisdom of the universe. It has the power to cure every disease that man has created or will create in the future. The Spiritual Light has the power to cure us at this very moment. All that is needed is our faith and trust and a complete surrendering to its healing energy.

Place yourself in a comfortable position so that the spine is erect. It is better to sit than to lie down if you have a tendency to fall asleep. Concentrate gently with eyes closed or partially open at a point between the eyebrows, the will center in man. Take several long, deep, rhythmic breaths; tense the entire body and then totally relax. Do this several times until you feel calmer. Now visualize White Light as a beam over your head descending on you, then enveloping your body.

As the White Light bathes you, visualize it becoming more and more brilliant. As it increases in brilliance, see it penetrating your body to the core of your being until every cell is saturated with healing light. Feel this light in every thought and feeling right down to the core of your body. As you are conscious of the Light permeating every particle of your being, offer a prayer or affirmation to the White Light that you are being healed. Feel that the address is to God Himself—which it is. You may pray: "Oh Divine White Light, heal me of all maladies in body, mind and soul." Then affirm in which specific direction you wish the healing to take place. No matter what ailment, thought or feeling is troubling you, pray that the healing may be concentrated in that area. Now see the diseased bodily area, thought or emotion being purified and converted in the White Light to a pure radiance. If it is physical healing you desire, visualize the affected area being converted into a radiant healthy one. See that state of perfection and do not let anything deflect you from wholeness and perfect health.

Through prolonged negativity we have created any undesirable conditions that may exist in our bodies, minds and souls. It may take time to recreate the perfect counterpart, but if we continue to visualize the perfect manifestation being molded by the White Light of Spirit, it will happen. As surely as the earth moves around the sun you can know you will be able to create your desired goal. It is not only a matter of faith; it is spiritual law—it cannot fail if the proper, sustained attitude and concentration is present.

If you are asking for a quality, feel that the negative one is being converted into the opposite, positive one. If you are trying to overcome sadness, then visualize the White Light converting that sadness into joy. See yourself transformed in the White Light. Behold yourself smiling from your soul with each cell of the body dancing in merriment. Hold that image of yourself throughout the day and feel that the White Light is with you helping you to manifest your newfound joy in all circumstances of life. Try this method for whatever quality you wish to manifest and you will achieve the desired results.

MEDITATION ON COLOR

The White Light is the all-powerful healing energy of God. Practice the White Light healing meditation: then continue by using a specific color ray. If you want to overcome fear and develop courage, feel that the White Light is converting all fear into bravery. Saturate yourself with orange. Let the Orange Ray sustain you and fill you with all the confidence you need to perform any task or gain any desire in your life. Should you have lung trouble, feel the orange strengthening and rebuilding your lungs. Hold the image that you are now healed of all respiratory difficulties. Learn the different relationships between color and bodily areas, mental qualities, and spiritual transcendence and use this knowledge in your meditations in order to perfect your being on all levels. Millions have done this in the past and millions will do so in the future, so take advantage of the divine science. It is being proven every day and it will work for us if we will give it an opportunity.

COLOR BREATHING

Practice the preliminary instructions in the meditation of the White Light until you feel calmness. Once the breath and emotions start to come under control, practice breathing in for a count of six, holding for a count of six then exhaling for a count of six. The count can be changed to suit one's needs but it should be the same for each phase of the breath so it is equal in duration.

Now visualize a glowing ball of White Light appearing before you. As you inhale feel that the rays of the White Light are entering your nostrils and lungs. Mentally direct the energy to the required area. Direct it to the heart for emotional problems; to the mind for negative thoughts; and to any bodily area that is distressed. If the area that is holding the negative emotion and thoughts is known, bathe that area as well.

During the phase of holding the breath, visualize and feel that the energy is saturating a particular area. As you exhale, hold the vibration of the color in the required area. Try to feel as you are exhaling that the negative, dark vibrations are being exhaled out of your lungs and nostrils and are being purified and transformed in the ball of brilliant White Light. Look for any dark, muddy vibrations that may be left inside you and see them being transformed in the radiant White Light that you are holding in the area for healing. Repeat the process again and again until you see and feel that the White Light is becoming brighter and brighter, converting all negativity into positive truth.

Practice the specific color ray designated for different qualities and ailments until you feel that your consciousness is saturated with the healing vibration of color. Visualize the required color becoming brighter and more radiant with each breath. Feel that the purity of color is changing all muddy negative vibrations into its transforming perfect vibration. The pure energy of color has now converted all inharmonious places into positive functioning areas. Carry that color and the positive manifestation that it has produced with you throughout the day. Let the vibration of the White Light and color be a beacon light to you in all phases and circumstances of your life.

SUNLIGHT AND ARTIFICIAL RAYS FROM LAMPS

More powerful than color from a pigment source is the energy from a radiant light source. The energy of color from a pigment is secondary energy as it is the reflected rays that are not absorbed by a material. Radiant color is direct energy from the source. Sunlight is the radiant energy of the sun, the direct manifestation of the sun itself. In the same way colored light bulbs and lights when shone through colored filters are radiant energy and have a much more powerful effect on consciousness than color received from a pigment. A colored bulb in a room is more powerful than the energy received from the color of the walls.

In using colored lights and filters for healing we must first establish where the problem lies and the best way to treat it. For those who have developed clairvoyant sight or if you look through Kilner screens, problem areas appear as dark patches in the etheric aura. Once the problem area is located, find the chakra center that controls that area and bathe its center with the energy of the required color.

In the cases of burns or other surface problems, bathe the area directly with the colored light. A hundred-watt bulb or direct sunlight can be used as the source of light to shine through the required colored filter. If it is possible to use direct sunlight, then the effect will be better than with an artificial source.

Color is a very subtle but also a powerful tool and should be used with sensitivity and respect. In the beginning, small exposures to color with attention to both intensity and time should be applied. Several minutes is sufficient at first. As the treatments progress and with sensitive observation of the patient's reactions you will be able to add or decrease time and intensity for better effect.

The function of all healing is to stimulate and unblock the flow of the inner life force to bring about improvement. All methods are, in principle, trying to stimulate the natural healing energies within so that the inharmonious vibrations may be able to oscillate into their natural, healthy vibrating frequency. Everything in the human organism responds to color in one way or another. When the right color is found and administered at the appropriate time and place with the right attitude on the part of patient and healer, a spontaneous healing takes place.

COLOR-CHARGED WATER

Take a glass and fill it with pure spring water; put the desired colored filter on top and place the contents in the sun. Leave the glass of water in the sunlight for at least one hour. The energy of the sun's rays will transmit the energy or vibration of the color into the water. This principle is similar to the method used in preparing Bach flower remedies. The flower heads are cut and placed in a dish of water and are left floating on the water in the sun. The healing essences of the flowers are absorbed into the water and later administered to the patient. After preparing the color-charged water it should then be refrigerated and sipped as required. Since the colors at the blue end of the spectrum are cooling and anti-septic they can be kept for seven to ten days in hot or cold weather without losing their properties. The color-solarized water at the red end of the spectrum should be changed every two days in warm weather and ten to fourteen days in cold weather. Sip the water throughout the day whenever you feel the need for its healing properties. Just a couple of tablespoons of charged water is sufficient.

Placing food for a few moments in the sunlight just before eating it is a good practice as it helps to recharge and purify the food. The color-solarizing method for water can be used for food as well.

FOODS AND THEIR COLOR ESSENCES

Mankind assimilates the seven color energies through his diet by the process of metabolism. The plant receives pure sunlight to bring about growth. The color rays are contained within the plants' energy and some plants have more of one color than others. Mankind, through the process of digestion, utilizes the color vibrations found within the various plants.

In order to be healthy we need to balance our diets so that we receive all the colors. If we are lacking in one our bodies will be out of balance and we will suffer from nutritional deficiencies. The body will continue to crave food and no matter how much we eat we will not be satisfied until we ingest the needed deficient color. This is one explanation of why so many are overweight.

If we do not receive the needed color, then disease will result. If we are deficient in violet, for example, we will be deficient in vitamin D. Each vitamin vibrates to a color. Vitamin A is yellow, vitamin B is red and orange, vitamin C is lemon, vitamin D is violet, vitamin E is scarlet or magenta and vitamin K is indigo. The foods that vibrate to red, orange and yellow are alkaline in effect. Blue, indigo and violet foods are acidic in effect and green foods are neutral being neither alkaline nor acid.

Very often we can recognize the vibrational color of certain elements due to the physical color we perceive through the sense of sight, but this is not always the case. Potatoes, for example, are brown or red and white in color but their vibrational color is blue. A person eating potatoes will experience the effect of the blue vibration. Prunes and figs contain the yellow energy, despite their outwardly dark color. Every element has an innate intelligence and color vibration and if we can become sensitive to these vibrations we will learn how they may be useful to us for our physical and mental well-being. Let us look at the color vibrations of certain foods.

Red Foods: Most red-skinned fruits and vegetables: cherries, red currants, red plums, strawberries, radishes, red cabbage, beets (roots and tops), red peppers, tomatoes, watercress, watermelon, meat.

Orange Foods: Most orange-skinned fruits and vegetables: peaches, tangerines, cantaloupes, mangos, persimmons, apricots, oranges, pumpkins, carrots.

Yellow Foods: Golden corn, yellow peppers, yams, parsnips, banana squash, lemons, bananas, pineapples, marrow, grapefruit, honeydew melons, and most yellow-skinned fruits and vegetables.

Green Foods: Most green fruits, vegetables and leafy greens do not have an acid or alkaline reaction.

Blue Foods: Blue-skinned fruits like blueberries, bilberries, plums, potatoes, asparagus, fish and veal.

Indigo Foods: Use both the blue and violet foods.

Violet Foods: Blackberries, purple grapes, beet tops, purple broccoli, eggplant.

GEM THERAPY

Gems are very pure in color. They are concentrated and undiluted sources of energy. They contain within them the same color rays as the planets in our solar system, but with less power. Like the planets, gems can affect human behavior physically, mentally, emotionally and spiritually. By placing gems next to the skin, their healing essences are taken into the body to help in various ailments. Gems can also be placed in water, alcohol or oil and allowed to sit for seven days until their energy saturates the substance. The medium in which the gem was placed then has very powerful healing properties. One drop of this liquid can be mixed with water and given as a treatment.

Red   — Rubies manifest the Red Ray.
Orange — Pearls carry the vibration of the Orange Ray.
Yellow — Coral gives off the vibration of the Yellow Ray.
Green   — Emeralds vibrate the Green Ray.
Blue   — Moonstones release the cooling Blue Ray.
Indigo   — Diamonds give off the Indigo Ray.
Violet   — Sapphires carry the Violet Ray.

COLOR AND CHEMICAL ELEMENTS

When an element undergoes a process of combustion or vaporization the acceleration in the motion of the electrons of the element causes a color to be emitted. Fraunhofer Lines is a term used to indicate the specific bands of colors emitted when an element is heated. By knowing the color characteristics of the elements it is possible to bring about the proper chemical balances in our bodies without using harmful chemical drugs which invariably contain an imbalance of color.

Red: Cadmium, Hydrogen, Krypton and Neon.

Orange: Aluminum, Antimony, Arsenic, Boron, Calcium, Copper, Helium, Selenium, Silicon and Xenon.

Yellow: Carbon, Glucinum, Iridium, Magnesium, Molybdenum, Osmium, Palladium, Platinum, Rhodium, Ruthenium, Sodium, Tin and Tungsten.

Lemon: Cerium, Germanium, Gold, Iodine, Iron, Lanthanum, Neodymium, Phosphorus, Praseodymium, Samarium, Scandium, Silver, Sulphur, Thorium, Titanium, Uranium, Vanadium, Yttrium and Zirconium.

Green: Barium, Chlorine, Kashmirium, Nitrogen, Radium, Tellurium, and Thallium.

Turquoise: Chromium, Columbium, Fluorine, Mercury, Nickel, Tantalum and Zinc.

Blue: Caesium, Indium, Lead and Oxygen.

Indigo: Bismuth, Ionium, Lead and Polonium.

Violet: Actinium, Cobalt, Gallium and Niton.

Purple: Bromine, Europium, Gadolxnium and Terbium.

Magenta: Irenium, Lithium, Potassium, Rubidium and Strontium.

Scarlet: Argon, Dysprosium Erbium, Holmium, Lutecium, Manganese, Thulium and Ytterbium.

I am the breath of virtue

Divine qualities flow through me

My tongue speaks kindness and goodness

My ears hear only the sweetness of truth

My eyes see only the God in all

My will and understanding work for the Will of God

My feet and hands work for the Glory of God

My heart gives unselfishly to all

Calmness and patience rule the day for me

Everyday and everyway I live my life filled with the gifts of
the angels of colors.

Bibliography

Amber, R.B. *Color Therapy*, Firma K.L. Mukhopadhyay, Calcutta, India, 1964.

Avalon, Arthur (Sir John Woodroffe). *The Serpent Power*, Dover Publications Inc., New York, N.Y., 1974.

Chinmoy, Sri. *Kundalini, The Mother Power*, Agni Press, Jamaica, New York, 1974.

Clark, Linda A. *The Ancient Art of Color Therapy*, Devin-Adair Co., Old Greenwich, Conn., 1975.

_____. *Health, Youth and Beauty Through Color Breathing*, Celestial Arts, Millbrae, Calif., 1976.

Colville W.J. *The Human Aura and the Significance of Color*, Health Research, Mokelumne Hill, Calif., 1970.

Fülöp, René-Miller. *The Saints that Moved the World*, Collier Books, New York, N.Y., 1962.

Ghadiali, Col. Dinshah P., M.Sc. *Spectro-Chrome-Metry Encyclopedia*, Volumes 1, 2, 3, Spectro-Chrome Institute, Malaga, N.J., 1939.

Hills, Norah. *You Are a Rainbow*, University of the Trees Press, Boulder Creek, Calif., 1979.

Hunt, Roland T. *The Seven Keys to Colour Healing*, C.W. Daniel Co., Ltd., London, England, 1971.

Johnston, Charles. *The Yoga Sutras of Patanjali,* Stuart and Watkins, London, England, 1968.

Ketcham, Howard. *Color (Its Theory and Application),* International Correspondence Schools, Scranton, Pennsylvania, 1956.

Leadbeater, Charles W. *The Chakras,* Adyar: The Theosophical Publishing House, London, England, 1927; rpt as Quest Book, 1972.

M. The Gospel of Sri Ramakrishna, Sri Ramakrishna Math, Mylopore, Madras, India. Sixth printing, 1974.

MacIvor, Virginia and LaForest, Sandra. *Vibrations,* Samuel Weiser, Inc., New York, N.Y., 1979.

Mayer, Gladys. *Colour and Healing,* New Knowledge Books, Sussex, England. Fourth printing, 1974.

Ott, John N. *Health and Light,* Devin-Adair Co., Old Greenwich, Conn., 1973.

Ouseley, S.G.J. *The Power of the Rays,* L. N. Fowler Co. Ltd., London, England. Fourth Printing, 1963.

_____. *The Science of the Aura,* L.N. Fowler Ltd., London, England. Eleventh Printing, 1975.

Saint Teresa of Avila. *The Autobiography of St. Teresa of Avila,* translated and edited by E. Allison Peers. A Doubleday Image Book, Garden City, New York, 1960.

_____. *Interior Castle,* translated and edited by E. Allison Peers. A Doubleday Image Book, Garden City, New York, 1961.

Saint Thérèse of Lisieux, *The Autobiography of St. Thérèse of Lisieux,* translation by John Beevers. A Doubleday Image Book, Garden City, New York, 1957.

Yogananda, Paramahansa. *The Autobiography of a Yogi,* Self-Realization Fellowship, 3880 San Rafael Ave., Los Angeles, Calif. 90065. Eleventh printing, 1971.

Yukteswar, Swami Sri. *The Holy Science,* Self-Realization Fellowship, 3880 San Rafael Ave., Los Angeles, Calif. 90065. Seventh printing, 1972.

CREATIVE THOUGHT REMEDIES
by Alex Jones

Creative Thought Remedies is a powerful aid for those who want to rediscover their inner beauty and remove undesirable traits from their characters.

Many people have the desire to transform themselves into successful, radiant beings but find it difficult to overcome deeply entrenched habits. They struggle for a while, then fall back into self-defeating patterns.

Creative Thought Remedies is a workbook that will help you guide your energies so that you may become successful in your undertakings and realize that you are pure love, peace, health and happiness.

TOPICS INCLUDED:

WHAT PROMOTES AND WHAT DIMINISHES JOYOUS LIVING—A study of the origins of life-promoting and life-diminishing processes and how to deal with situations in life from a state of control rather than slavery.

WINNING AS A WAY OF LIFE—Learn the self-enriching attitudes necessary to overcome limiting and destructive habits.

TRANSFORMING UNDESIRABLE HABITS—Discover how to overcome fear through courage; overindulgence by self-control; anger with wisdom; restlessness by way of calmness; jealousy and hate via love; and more.

RELATIONSHIPS—Discover guidelines for a creative, enriching relationship and attitudes necessary to maintain that relationship.

VIRTUES—Learn the art of self-love, self-confidence; happiness under all conditions, and the rules for successful living.

PERSONAL CHART—A unique system to help you record your tendencies and find out who and what you are and the steps necessary to build a solid foundation for the change necessary to become what you want to be.

Cassette Tapes For Meditation and Relaxation
by Alex Jones

Instrumental Music

KALI'S DREAM   *Piano*

Joyful piano melodies ripple like cool mountain streams, and the moods change colors like the seasons. Alex Jones is well known as a New Age musician whose pure and crystal-clear solo piano compositions evoke a subtle and beautiful feeling that just isn't present in much popular music. The music expresses the creative play and the depth of Nature in a way that touches the peace and beauty within each listener.

AWAKE AND DREAMING   *Piano & Synthesizer*

Devotional in nature, these simple melodies soothe the aching of your soul with a mellow blend of piano and synthesizer. The nine cuts are like gentle lullabies that enfold you in loving peace. The softer side of electronic music, perfect after a tiring day.

LOKAS: SPHERES OF PEACE   *Piano*

Celestial piano melodies that are truly a feast for the ears and upliftment for the soul. Performed in a classical style, the ten selections flow gently and slowly and will align a stressed mind and body with its calming space. The soothing music will carry the listener on a transforming voyage of peace.

PRANAVA   *Flute & Harp*

The flute and harp selections interlace to create a musical tapestry that is tranquil and yet uplifting. All selections have a depth of devotion and peace that is unparalleled. The ten compositions are very quiet and gentle. Such is their sublime simplicity that the effect on the nervous system is one of instantaneous calm. The penetrating music truly brings one's essence into balance and harmony.

INSIDE THE HOLLOW   *Piano & Synthesizer*

By popular request we are making available as a solo instrumental cassette the background music from *Infinite Directions*. From Side 1 you will feel the expansive music of the piano and synthesizer awaken unexplored realms of inner consciousness. Side 2 is devotional in nature, and the piano and synthesizer move the heart to the gentleness of love.

Guided Meditations

ANGELS OF COLOR & SOUND   *Guided Meditation (Narration) with Piano Background*

Angels of Color is a guided meditation on the seven rays emanating from the seven chakras or spinal centers in the body. With this tape each chakra will be stimulated by listening to inspiring musical selections and narration that are in resonance with each chakra. By following the guided color meditation, the seven rays of divine qualities—vitality, courage, joy, love, peace, intuition, and soul realization—will be awakened.

Angels of Sound is solo piano compositions that bring tranquility to a restless mind.

INFINITE DIRECTIONS   *Guided Meditation (Narration) with Piano Background*

Two guided meditations. Side 1 is a visualization exercise to help one feel an expansion of consciousness. The mind's true nature is Cosmic Consciousness and is not limited to the conscious or subconscious state. With the aid of this visualization one can sense that one is the infinite, omnipresent, limitless soul.

Side 2 is a meditation on self-love and confidence. Through this visualization exercise one can begin to feel a connection with the Creator and understand that one is a child of God. Re-identification with the beauty within opens the door to all positive expressions and the growth of confidence and self-respect.

IMAGINATION'S DOOR   *Affirmations (Narration) with Piano Background*

Affirmations work on the principle of magnetism. When revolving our will-power around a thought, a force field is set up drawing within its circle that which is being affirmed. Through the proper use of affirmations in this cassette we can realize total health and our own divinity.

For information about ordering books and tapes, please write to:

Alex Jones
Eastern Gate Publishing Inc.
P.O. Box 1485
Front Royal, VA 22630